think yourself thin

To my cosmic family...my amazing husband John Demartini, my wonderfully supportive friends Della Rounick, Deborah Gray, Jennifer Fox, Shelley Rahim and my sister Janet Cook. You all light up my life.

think yourself thin

how to achieve your perfect weight
by using the power of your mind

Athena Starwoman

First published in Australia in 2004 by
New Holland Publishers (Australia) Pty Ltd
Sydney • Auckland • London • Cape Town

14 Aquatic Drive Frenchs Forest NSW 2086 Australia
218 Lake Road Northcote Auckland New Zealand
86 Edgware Road London W2 2EA United Kingdom
80 McKenzie Street Cape Town 8001 South Africa

10 9 8 7 6 5 4 3 2 1

National Library of Australia Cataloguing-in-Publication Data:

Starwoman, Athena.
Think yourself thin: how to achieve your perfect weight by using the power
of your mind.

ISBN 1 74110 112 3.

1. Weight loss—Psychological aspects. I. Title.

153.85

Publishing Manager: Robynne Millward
Printer: McPherson's Printing Group, Victoria
Front cover image by Verko Photography, New York
Back cover image by Mark Bramley, courtesy of ACP Publishing

CONTENTS

Reaching and maintaining your perfect weight with this guide is quick and stress-free. It involves no drugs, dietary supplements or strenuous exercise.

Introduction
Start To Lose Weight and Begin to Love Yourself Again

Losing weight by using the psychic power of your mind begins with faith and then quickly becomes a reality.

Athena

Nobody jumps enthusiastically out of bed in the morning and thinks to themselves, 'I am going to eat like a pig today and get as fat and lumpy as I can.' Yet, that is exactly what many people end up doing. Statistics reveal that nearly 85 per cent of Americans and 56 per cent of Australians consider themselves overweight and hate the fact that they are. These figures also appear to be increasing every year. Then why do some people seem to be their own worst enemy and set about doing all the wrong things when it comes to creating their own body image?

I believe one reason is that they have forgotten about the unbelievable power of their own minds. This power holds the key to their own inner abilities to create what they desire. Naturally, it is hard to believe in your own mind's powers when you are unhappy and overweight, but, if you've tried every type of diet and failed, then it's likely that what is blocking your dieting success exists within; in the way you are thinking.

Trust me when I tell you that once you start developing the power of your own mind and tap into your own psychic mind powers, you can immediately turn your life in a happier and more powerful direction. Once you rekindle your own mind's willpower, you will be more consistent and disciplined because using your thoughts constructively will build up your confidence and willpower. As a consequence, many people have lost a lot of weight in a week and kept it off indefinitely simply by mastering their own inner powers.

So as you turn the pages of this book you will find that it describes the simplest and easiest weight loss program in the world. All you have to do is let me help you tune into your own mental and psychic mental powers through my own mind's psychic and mental powers. Working together, we will re-train your way of thinking and the pounds and kilos will fall off as you start to mentally 'think yourself thin'. Once you tap into your mind's psychic and mental powers, you will not need as much food as you required in the past. You will soon have a different attitude, taste and desire for food, and for everything else too— because you will be thinking more constructive thoughts and creating a different attitude towards food and your self-image. Soon, like magic, any past over-indulgences you had when it comes to eating, or other bad habits, will be transformed into healthier, more positive traits.

As you embark upon your journey of the mind, always remember: In life, everything is possible for those who believe. So let me help you discover and use the mental magic within you. This will give you unlimited power and the mind powers to live the life of your dreams and get into perfect physical shape!

Chapter One
How the Mind Powers Weight Loss Program Works

What the mind thinks about, it brings about! Athena

Do you believe in psychic energy and the power of the mind? I do. Whilst writing this book, I used my thought power and placed a mental energy around every word as I wrote with my thoughts, so my mind's energy is resonating within each and every page. This mental energy is directed in a way that it will begin to flow towards you from the moment you come into contact with this book! If you stop and tune into your senses right now, you may even feel the mind power's energy flowing through you as you hold the book in your hands. What would this feel like? Well, do you feel your heart beat a little faster? Alternatively, is there a tingling sensation in your fingers? Maybe your mind suddenly feels calmer or more focused or you are feeling more dreamy than usual? If you cannot notice any obvious reaction to the mental powers in this book, do not worry. It sometimes takes a little practice and fine-tuning to recognise the subtle feelings of mental attunement—such as the emotions you feel when you listen to music or see wonderful sunsets. But if you feel nothing, relax and just take in the words before you. These mental feelings or sensations will come to you soon. In the meantime, enjoy this moment, where you are reaching out to 'feel the power in the air around and within you'. This invisible power perpetually surrounds each and every one of us, but very few tap into it because they don't even know about it.

Understanding and being in tune with your mind powers will enable you to control your thoughts and desires. You will be able to monitor your moods and your appetite, thereby replacing negative feelings or hunger through boredom (which can lead to binge eating), with positive thoughts about yourself and visions of being slim. In order to do this I will describe to you in this book various tools and techniques to use to get your psychic energy flowing and to develop your willpower. Remember that mind powers can help your wishes come true, so this is also an ideal time to make a wish. You can help your wish along by touching the Lucky Magic Star on the opposite page.

Lucky Magic Star

Let your mental power thinking begin with some wish-making. Place your right hand on the Lucky Magic Star to start the mental magic flowing. Make a wish for something—anything—you desire to happen in the future. You can wish for something easy to fulfill, or you can make your wish as wonderful, crazy or unbelievable as you like. You may even choose to go as far as to wish, 'I'm going to marry a prince and live in a castle!' Think the wish and...that's all there is to it!

Once the Lucky Magic Star is energised by your special touch, it will send your wish-message out to the universe, and the forces of mental thinking will begin working for you. (Once you have made your wish, keep an open mind. Your wish may not be fulfilled literally—let's face it, there are only so many royal families and so many actual princes—but you may find your own 'prince', a man who behaves like a prince, and who treats you like a princess. And, when compared to your present quarters, the new house you move into may well be a 'castle'.)

Use the Lucky Magic Star anytime you desire to make something happen or have a wish come true. Remember, now that you have started the mental magic flowing, it is unwise for you to allow anyone else to touch this book, in case their mind's energy conflicts with yours and depletes the power of the lucky star's magic. Remember: Why save your wishes just for birthdays when you blow out the candles? Get into the habit of making a wish every day and use the Lucky Magic Star to help make your wishes come true.

Lucky Magic Star

Conjuring Up Your Willpower

The mind power energy I have placed within the energy field of this book—the flow of energy that is held between each page—includes the magic energy of increased willpower. This mind power energy will assist you in many dramatic and subtle ways and it is yours to claim and own simply by believing in it. I have always believed in the power of my own mind—it is what has helped me lead a magical life. Experience has taught me that when you believe in your own powers, amazing things can occur—sometimes even miracles!

With the assistance of this book, the mind power energy and the empowered energy flow it contains, you can begin to tap into the higher-minded, soul-connected willpower part of yourself. This invisible part of you is immortal and is free to operate beyond the boundaries of your everyday mortal limitations of time and space. It can help you rise above any earthbound temptations or weaknesses too.

Sometimes, in order to tap into this more powerful side of yourself, you need a little help. Therefore, to assist you in losing weight, gaining confidence and developing willpower, look into the photograph of my eyes attached to this book. When I had this psychically energised photograph taken of my eyes, I projected my own psychic powers out towards the camera, directing my mind power energies towards the person who looked into this photograph. The way I did this was to project a message out from my mind when the camera clicked—a message about you and sent to you, so take it as your own: *I love myself. I love the way that I look. I am not hungry. I have no desire to eat anything that is not serving my health and my beauty. In fact, fatty, rich food repulses me. Now, when I eat I will desire only healthy light meals that nourish and energise my health and vitality.*

This photograph of my eyes holds all my focused mental powers and represents my mind's message to you to gain power within yourself. It is designed to be used as a tool to remind you to believe in yourself and in your own willpower. Each time you look into my eyes, this empowering message is subliminally passed on to you. When you look into the photo, my message will enter your mind's thoughts. Once your mind has become accustomed to receiving this message of your own mind's strengths, you will not need to glance at my eyes any more. However, it is only until you firmly inculcate this message into your own consciousness that it will become an automatic part of your thinking. This photo is your reminder to think healthy thoughts. It also represents your psychic connection to me. Use my photo to remind you to think differently, to eat wisely and to develop your own mind and mental powers. Use it whenever you need to remind yourself of your own mind's incredible powers!

To begin using this photograph to its full advantage, photocopy it several times and strategically place the copies at selected and logical locations around your home or workplace. Select anywhere you feel the temptation could arise for you to eat and forget about your true desires. For example, it may help you to avoid food if you place a copy of my psychically energised photo on the door of your refrigerator—this way you can use the psychic and mental powers in the photo to deter you from eating. Once the photos are positioned, you then need to look into my eyes as often as is practical to ensure that your own inner powers, combined with my powers, are working for you. When you look at my photo, clear your thoughts and actually think to yourself: 'I am opening myself up to tapping into my own and Athena's psychic powers.' At any given moment you can just glance at the energised psychic photo now and then or, if you feel intuitively prompted to do so, sit in front of it for five to twenty minutes at a time. However, psychic energy exchange and mental energy flow does not rely on the 'time' you actually spend attuning to it, because this type of energy is an imponderable essence. All you need to remember is that it can be relaxing, comforting and inspirational to meditate and let yourself absorb as much psychic energy as possible.

Psychic exchanges work in an instant. Time does not exist on the psychic levels of exchange. Our human nature simply feels more worthy, receptive or comfortable when it knows we have invested a lot of time (or at least sufficient time), energy and focus into a pursuit, and we like to feel we deserve the rewards it offers. Parents who have strong work ethics have often created this belief in their children, because they have had these beliefs since their childhood, and believe that what they got out of any situation was what they put into it. Spending more time connecting with the psychic energy flow will work best for these people. Therefore, the amount of time a person needs to attune to my psychic and mental message will differ, with some only needing to glance occasionally to make a close connection.

The most important action of all is to follow and trust your own inner instinct as to the amount of time you spend attuning to my eyes in the psychically energised photograph. Not only do you decide *when* to look at my photo, but also for *how long*. All I recommend is that, as well as taking as many glances at the photo as possible and making eye-to-eye contact with it, you spend at least one or two sittings a day (morning and evening) doing your own psychic imaging. This ensures that you get that certain inner mental feeling that you have connected to my psychic energy flow and are using it to create your dream existence. Also remember that whenever you make this psychic connection through looking at my photo, there should be no effort involved. Psychic energy and mental exchange should be effortless. It is an invisible flow of ease, not a forced feeling. If you feel tense or pressured during these psychic connection times, in any fashion at all, it is advisable to wait until another time when you are more psychically or emotionally receptive.

When your mind is open and receptive, it is very easy for my psychic message to be transferred over to you. You are likely to feel some faint or powerful sensation when this occurs. There may also be a tingling feeling as the electromagnetic wave energy moves around. Sometimes you may feel a sense of calmness or tranquility come over you, as you move from your everyday mind state into a higher, more relaxed, visionary mind state.

You can do your psychic connecting with my photo at any time of the day or night. Similar to radio or television waves passing through the air, psychic energy is always there and available, but it does take some attention from you to 'tune into it'.

For those readers who have practiced meditation, opening up to psychic energy may come easier. The sensation you will experience when making your psychic connection with my energised photo is likely to be similar to a state of mind you might sometimes experience or feel when you are meditating. Some experience this higher state when resting or even sleeping.

Attuning to psychic energy depends on finding the key to tuning into it. I am providing the psychically and mentally energised photos of my eyes to assist you in this attunement. Once you have experienced the state of psychic connection and know what it feels like, you will be able to recreate this psychically empowered state for yourself, unaided by me. When this 'psychic connection' or attunement with me takes place, your own willpower will automatically be empowered and the desire for food will be over-ridden by your own energised state of mind and increased willpower. In some cases where this connection between you and me is very strong, after a very short time my psychic and mental message will become your own mind's message. Then you will no longer need to use my psychically energised photo at all. Powerful willpower will be your own, and you will no longer need my support and encouragement. You will learn to summon your own psychic powers and mental influences, and put them to work at will in other areas of your life. When you know how to summon up your willpower, it is available to you whenever you desire.

One of the greatest advantages in mastering your own mind powers is that, as you begin to see the results you are attaining, you realise that you are running your life and not succumbing to your desires. This gives you a feeling of pride about your own strength of character. Now you love yourself for what you have achieved. Once you acknowledge your accomplishment, this helps to keep you on a healthy diet indefinitely.

Once your mind is in control of your body, when you do eat you will only feel the desire to eat lightly, and you will only want food that is very healthy and good for you. Therefore, the additional magic or ingredient to this program is that you naturally develop the desire to eat lightly and healthily. You will not only lose weight but you will also get the benefit of desiring to only eat nutritious foods.

Therefore when people ask me whom I recommend to give them a personal psychic reading, I often respond: 'You can give yourself the best reading!' No matter how far you travel the planet searching for someone to look into your future, the truth is that you can be your own best tomorrow teller. Just by picking up this book, and reading it this far, you have shown you have the interest and the natural psychic ability to begin to access your own inner truth and strengths. Working with me, you are commencing to attune to your own psychic powers and have started working with them to make your future journey a journey of joy, creativity, power and self-fulfillment.

Chapter Two
How Your Mind Affects Your Life

You can change your entire life when you change the way you think—especially when it comes to your body's shape and size.
Athena

How does making a shift in mental thinking, glancing at mind-energised photographs and making all kinds of wishes help you to lose weight and generally live a better life? I believe every thought, emotion and attitude you have plays a major role in the way your body looks and feels and how you live your life. When you are happy and radiant, you look and appear bigger and brighter and think grander thoughts. When you are happy, people tell you that you 'stand ten feet tall', while when you're miserable, depressed or feeling sorry for yourself, you seem to shrink into your skin. At these times, it is as if you are being pulled inward by some perverse form of gravity. While you may not see the dark cloud surrounding you, people around you will point it out with comments like, 'You're sure in a dark mood today'. At times like this, our view of life, ourselves, our potential, our plans, our desires and the driving forces that help create a fulfilling existence, all shrivel up as well. At these times we dwell on our problems and forget to look for opportunities. These are the times when we 'think small!'

Many experiments have been done to ascertain how much our thoughts affect us. One experiment, conducted by the Esalen Institute in California between 1992 and 1993, came up with some amazing results. Participants were asked to learn and use mind exercises to reshape their bodies. During this program, many were able to achieve measurable goals of change in their appearance, such as the perception of being taller. In another experiment conducted by Harvard University, elderly men were asked to envisage themselves as young during the three-day study. By the end, many felt much younger than they were—some even up to twenty years![1]

Of course, the genetic predisposition of our parents and grand-parents plays a major role in creating our body shape. Some may even say that it is the genetic make-up and thinking patterns passed down from our ancestors that create most of the things about us too—possibly even effecting our body shape. Thoughts affect us in more ways than we know, and we inherit attitudes and/or thoughts from our parents as well. Our ancestors, themselves, were the recipients of a long line of mental and emotional coding which was passed down from their ancestors, which has been now passed down to us. If we don't have the same body shape as our parents, we probably inherited our shape, thinking patterns and attitudes from an ancestor of generations ago—either genetically or psychologically. So, contrary to the belief that 'we are what we eat', it is 'what we think' that truly spins our wheels! Our thoughts direct us towards our daily dietary habits. They influence us so that we react or behave in specific ways, especially when it comes to being the perfect weight and size. It is our thoughts that direct us towards eating certain foods and eating less or more!

[1] (Sanders, Pete, A., 1999, *You are Psychic! The free soul method*, Prentice Hall & IBD)

Strange Things Can and Do Happen When You Change Your Way of Thinking

I speak from personal experience when I tell you that you can change your entire life when you change the way you think— especially when it comes to your body's shape and size. How your mind perceives your body makes a big impact on your physical image. By changing your attitude about yourself, you can break through your own inward conditioning. You do this when you make an effort to restructure and reprogram the thinking cycle of your innermost emotional and attitudinal patterns. This book is designed to help you access the power deep within you (and also the power that surrounds you out in the universe). This power within and around you—when used creatively—has the ability to reshape your body and soul into a new, vibrant, more fulfilled, complete and confident person.

Until the mind is treated, it is futile to attempt to treat the body.
Inspirational speaker, John Demartini

How Nature Uses Magic

Nature uses and plays with psychic and internal mind powers all the time. In most forms of life, both flora and fauna, the physical condition and shape are naturally attuned to, restructured and balanced with regularity, often as a means of survival or protection. Animals can change shape, colour and size according to their needs, at will. To an outsider, this process of nature can only be described as 'magical', when in fact it is just nature doing its job. Being able to blend in or stand out in nature is entirely a natural process in the animal kingdom. We humans seem to be far less adept at mastering the shape, condition and progress of our physical condition—or so it seems on the surface of things, at least!

Therefore, as we are also operating under nature, it is unwise to underestimate the power your mind wields over your body. There is a classic reference cited frequently in medical studies concerning a man who was accidentally locked in a freezer overnight. When he was found dead the next morning, he had all the physical characteristics associated with freezing to death, yet, amazingly, the freezer he had been locked in had not been turned on! His mind told him that he would freeze to death, and so he did!

Then there is the phenomenon known as phantom pregnancy, a state that defies most medical assessment. For no explicable reason, a woman's body suddenly believes it is pregnant and goes through the entire sequence of pregnancy starting at gestation. Trouble is, since there was no actual coupling of sperm and ovum, there is no baby forming within. So, although the woman believes she is full term, she does not deliver her 'baby'. Somehow, a subliminal belief in the psyche sent out an 'I'm pregnant' message to the reproductive system and this message was strong enough to fool the body itself!

Hypnosis, too, has shown how much autosuggestion influences our physical bodies. Under hypnosis, individuals with severe allergies can lose their sensitivity to the substance that normally incapacitates them. Under the influence of hypnosis, a person who is touched by an ice-cube who has been *told* is a hot coal, can believe they are suffering a real burn to the skin. He or she mentally experiences the same injury as would be received from being burnt by a hot smoldering coal.

Psychic and mind study research can teach us a lot about our human functioning and developmental possibilities. Few people are really aware of the incredible psychic and out-of-body experiences that are triggered by athletic performance, where individuals push themselves beyond the normal threshold of human endurance. Everybody, from the athlete to those who seldom or never exercise, can attain extraordinary abilities when they embark on a mind-exploring adventure.

People may not view what occurs to them or around them as a psychic experience. Instead, they may see it as some type of extraordinary breakthrough of their usual mode of operation or attainment. Dramatic transformations of the body and mind occur when we start to enter the realm of the higher mind—the 'psychic realm of operation'. It requires courage to embark upon a psychic and mental journey, for you are entering the realm of the inexplicable and unknown—the realm where things happen that nobody can explain.

As you can see from the examples above, the mind is capable of playing all sorts of tricks, and it is important that you realise this in order to control your weight. Many people have resigned themselves to weight gain because their mind has told them that they have a slow metabolic rate, which causes them to gain weight. But this mental construct is more a state of mind than a truism. The more you repeat this 'belief' to yourself, the more it will become true! What is required is that you make a shift in your consciousness and alter your metabolic rate anyway you want. You can do this by learning to use the hidden, and often untapped, power we have within us all—our mind's psychic power.

Chapter Three
Everyone is Psychic
—Even You!

Psychic phenomenon is occurring around us every minute of every day. Athena

I am extraordinarily blessed. I hail from a long line of mystics who valued their psychic gifts and encouraged me to develop my own extra-sensory focus. My grandmother was a famous psychic who totally believed in magic, and also a famous singer who sang the most extreme range of chords. Her powers in singing, she believed, stemmed from the fact that as she sang, she held a rose quartz crystal in her palm and let the power of the crystal empower her singing range.

Inheriting her mother's gifts, my mother was also exceptionally psychic. She would keep all the neighbours in our area well entertained with her ability to read their future just by holding their wedding rings in the palm of her hand. Even my sister, who is also an astrologer called Planet Janet, has an uncanny ability to pick people's star signs with incredible accuracy, just by simply looking at them! This, naturally, is a great party trick and one that I continually envy her for.

When I was a child, my mother suspected that I had inherited the family's psychic ability, and when I was three years old she was rewarded with all the proof she needed. It was a mild winter's day in Melbourne, Australia. As we munched on pastries at Patterson's Cake Shop, I announced in a loud voice to all the customers in the shop: 'I'm going to build a snowman tomorrow and play with a great big ball of snow and ice'. This was quite a departure for a normally timid child prone to attacks of asthma.

Not only did I say it once, but I kept repeating it parrot-fashion, because I was looking forward to the 'vision' of my adventures of the next day. As Melbourne's climate has seen snow only on very rare occasions, and as snow was not even a remote possibility at this time, this was quite a ridiculous statement as far as anyone listening was concerned. They all turned back to their business quite amused by such a childish outburst.

As it turned out, the next day snow fell heavily—enough for me to build my snowman. Later that day enormous hailstones, ones that actually caused damage to homes and cars, pelted the area. Out of these 'diamonds' from the sky, I made my ball of ice.

So, I found out early in life that I had a talent for tapping into the unknown. Having this insight inspired me to explore this talent and develop it further. For the past thirty years I have spent at least one hour a day practising my own psychic abilities. These daily practices have helped me keep slim and trim, meet my soulmate, develop my career to a high level of success, and to become financially independent. In this book, I will impart to you my secrets, which you too can use to get back to the body you were meant to have or to upgrade your existence in any way you wish!

If I Can Do It So Can You

Using psychic powers or insights to get what you want out of life is nothing new. Since ancient times, people have used their own psychic powers or consulted those they believed could see or manipulate the future. The prophets of the future were tribal medicine men and shamans, the wise women of Wicca, the soothsayers or oracles of ancient Rome, and 'tomorrow teller' gypsies. In our time, fortune-tellers take the form of psychic housewives who do readings 'on the side'; professional mystics, such as myself, whose predictions appear in newspapers, magazines or on television; and even computer software programmed to read the future. Someone claiming to be able to 'see into the future' can be found promoting their unique skills in just about any neighbourhood, community or city.

Many people are desperate to consult psychics about their love lives, prospects for wealth and, of course, health. Many who have consulted psychics claim the things they were told about their past and their future were extraordinarily accurate—frighteningly so. Psychics often 'know' about things that no one but you could possibly know about—not even your closest friend. But whether or not you are a believer in psychic abilities, most people have at some time encountered powerful psychic phenomena, even though they may not admit it or even realise it.

When psychic energy surrounds us, our lives often run a very unusual course and it can appear that fact is stranger than fiction. That is why many people tend to push away the psychic or mystical things that occur in their lives. They can't explain these things, so they either deny or ignore them, dismissing the psychic occurrence as coincidence or an accident of fate.

Whether because of the development of verbal communication or whatever else has occurred to block our psychic development, humankind has now become separated from its most blessed birthright—the ability to function on psychic levels of operation. Many people experience all kinds of difficulties because they are unaware of their own psychic experience and psychic states. Because humans have forgotten their psychic abilities doesn't mean psychic events have stopped occurring. There is psychic phenomena happening all around us at every minute of the day. Often the difference between the expert psychic and the ordinary person is that the psychic expert is practising and using their psychic energies all the time, while the ordinary person doesn't recognise his or her psychic powers. I hold the belief that psychic ability is inherent within all of us and that being psychic is not such a special gift after all. Just about anybody can access a psychic state—you probably do it all the time, unconsciously, without even realising it.

Science Has Proven That We All Possess Psychic Powers

Knowing as much as you can about your own psychic senses, or which psychic senses you are most proficient in, can make you much more efficient at using these abilities to reshape your life. An extensive biomedical, chemistry and brain science study of more than 100,000 people at the Massachusetts Institute of Technology (MIT) revealed that there are four psychic personality types—psychic feeling, psychic intuition, psychic hearing and psychic vision. The study concluded that no matter which type you are, if you practise certain simple exercises, you can tap into your limitless psychic abilities AT WILL.[2] It is also interesting to note that, contrary to the popular belief that women are the psychic sex, men are also equally as psychic as women. Women are just more open about their psychic expression than men.

Most of us tap into all of the four psychic senses at various times of our life, even if unconsciously. However, this research revealed that most individuals are usually stronger in one or two of these senses, and the other two can be dormant unless we actively set out to reconnect with them.

The Four Psychic Personality Types

Most people tap into the four psychic senses at some point in their life. As you read the outline of the four different psychic senses, you do not need to judge whether you have any, all, or none, of the senses—wait until you answer the quiz at the end of this chapter. This quiz will help you to determine which psychic senses you are most attuned to. What the psychic personality types will tell you is how to approach your diet and weight problems according to what category you are under.

[2] (Sanders, Pete, A., 1999, *You are Psychic! The free soul method*, Prentice Hall & IBD)

Psychic Feeling

This is the most common of all the psychic senses. You will recognise this psychic feeling in your solar plexus, the network of nerves found in the upper part of the stomach. The feeling of having butterflies in the stomach is often a symptom of this psychic sense. Psychic feeling hits our intuitive emotional areas. It attracts, assimilates and draws in the feelings of whoever or whatever is about. People with this 'psychic radar' pick up all kinds of information around them and can become very unhappy in a depressed environment. They can suffer from mood swings because their feeling levels are so sensitive. If you are this kind of person, you should definitely not associate with other people who have a negative outlook. You need to pick your associates most carefully and monitor the way you spend your time with them.

People with this psychic sense, who also wish to lose weight, are best to avoid spending time with people who sit around eating their way through the day (or eating their way through their emotional traumas). This is definitely not going to serve you well. Make friends with people who eat good food and follow a path to good health. Associate with people who have a positive attitude about their health and body. Do they order candy at the movies or do they take an apple with them? Do they have second helpings...or even thirds? Gradually remove these individuals from your life because they are likely to be having a negative influence upon you. Alternatively, get them on a healthy psychic regime too!

The benefit to this psychic feeling power is that it makes you highly creative, extremely attuned to other people, and very sensitive to the world around you. You can use this power to its highest benefit by exploring your creativity in ways that will improve your life. Get out the cookbooks and start finding recipes for low fat, delicious meals. A little extra effort and you can become slimmer and trimmer and flex your creative muscles while you're at it.

For this psychic type, the best advice for you, when faced with a situation where you feel compelled to eat, is to postpone the act of eating. Delaying eating can turn out to be the best diet of all for you. As a 'feeler', your emotions can change at a moment's notice. If you keep busy doing other things, something else is likely to come about in the meantime that will take you on another journey that leads you away from the refrigerator. Distractions work great for you when it comes to avoiding eating. Instead of munching on cookies or going back for second helpings, take the dog for a walk, tinker in the garden, or make some healthy food preserves (not of sugary fruits, but of wonderful, nutritious vegetables—this way you can start looking forward to a healthy 'treat' that you made yourself). Do whatever it takes to move away from thinking and feeling about food, to thinking and feeling about something—anything—else.

Some psychic feelers go to extremes when it comes to what they put in their bodies. If it isn't food they are eating, they may be popping pills, drinking sodas, or even going on binge diets or using tranquilizers of some sort to anaesthetise their desire. If this applies to you at times, do the total opposite of what you're feeling. Instead of popping a pill or taking a nap, get busy and go for walk or shop till you drop (but not in a supermarket or bakery!). Do an exercise you enjoy, like swimming or hiking through the glorious countryside. Do something that is out of the ordinary or different for you, because as it is said, 'if you keep doing the same old things, you will keep getting the same old results'.

Remember, psychic feeling is the most prevalent psychic sense around, so most people (or the majority of the population) are affected by its positives and negatives. This psychic sense is possibly one of the main reasons why so many people become overweight. Look at how the feelings of the following people affect their weight: Elizabeth Taylor, Liza Minnelli, Oprah Winfrey, John Travolta, Sarah Ferguson (Fergie), Rosie O'Donnell, Roseanne Barr, Elton John, Ricki Lake and Monica Lewinsky. In most cases, they are all in the 'feeling business'.

Psychic Intuition

Psychic intuition operates on the intellectual, calmer, more detached area of ourselves. It works more in a mental capacity rather than an emotional one. The physical area of the body associated with psychic intuition is the top of the head—the crown. Psychic intuitive people often suffer from headaches or need little sleep. If the sense is highly developed, those in contact with these people may even catch a glimpse of a glow, like an aura, coming out of their heads. My husband, who is an inspiration speaker, is a psychic intuitive. When he gives lectures, people in the audience often comment that they can see a golden light surrounding his head when he is speaking.

Psychic intuition occurs when the individual has a 'knowing' sense about things—they just *know* something is going to happen and they can't explain exactly why or how. What makes psychic intuitive people eat is when they go against their own inner knowledge or sense of what they should do. They know what they should do, but they let outside circumstances run their lives, instead of their intuitive promptings. Let's say you don't want to take care of the children, you're just not in the mood, and you need time for yourself to read, call a friend, or to just sit and vegetate! It's your time to be doing something for you, but school's out, you haven't made any plans, and you're stuck at home with the kids. This is when, because you're not living your own truth, but a lie to yourself, you will tend to binge on all the things you swore you'd never eat. It's like you're punishing yourself for not having your life in better order. Maybe you should have taken the kids to an amusement park or arranged for them to go to the movies with their friends? You feel torn down the middle. You know your real needs, but you aren't following them. These are the type of guilt trips the psychic intuitive lays upon themself, and guilt leads straight to the cookie jar. If you are an intuitive person you need to learn to read yourself and to know your needs and make sure they are met, if not all the time, then most of the time! The smoother your life runs, the less you'll overeat and the more you'll do things to take care of yourself and those around you. I don't have to tell you what those things are, or if you are not fulfilling yourself. You know what they are!

Heed your 'hunches'. They will probably turn out to be right! Trust that knowingness within you. Psychic intuitive individuals are often some of the most successful business people around. They are often not aware that their shrewd moves have been prompted from the fact that they are highly psychic beings. Psychic intuitive types include: Bill Gates, Jerry Seinfeld, Celine Dion, Hilary Clinton, Donald Trump, Al Pacino, Francis Ford Coppola, Madonna and Tiger Woods.

Psychic Hearing

Sometimes called clairaudience, this can be a very frightening psychic sense to have because it provides the person with a profound experience where they actually hear very clearly 'an inner voice'. The body area associated with the state of psychic hearing is located on either side of the head, above the ears. With psychic hearing, the individual can experience a sense that a message is being given to them by the spoken word—they actually hear a voice talking to them telling them certain information. This experience has often been depicted in religious stories and also, unfortunately, this higher psychic sense has often been mistaken for a lower-minded malady that is associated with schizophrenia or other mental problems. I have had this psychic hearing force affect me quite profoundly at various times and it has really made a big difference to my life—for the better. This experience occurred to me when I was woken up by the sound of a voice talking to me in 1988, telling me to make a move from Australia to New York. To ensure that it got its point across, the voice woke me three nights in a row. I listened to it and I went to New York three days later!

Surprisingly, psychic hearing is a very common psychic state, although many do not realise what is happening when it occurs, or think they are cracking up when they do. When someone has the psychic hearing sense, they sometimes not only receive psychic messages to themselves but also have the capacity to pick up psychic messages from others. Naturally hearing what other people are thinking can be very intimidating. You can be walking down the street and hear something in your own mind that are actually the thoughts of another person. This happened to me once in New York City and you should have heard some of the weird, kooky thoughts these diversified New Yorkers were having!

If you are a psychic hearer, you probably don't have a messy weight problem, but you can be somewhat out of shape. You are more often the body type with great calves, but a swollen tummy or cottage cheese thighs. You usually don't eat to ease any emotional angst—in fact, sometimes emotional angst makes you repelled by food—however, you may eat when you feel over-whelmed by work or by responsibility. Intensity is something that fuels you, and so you frequently are caught up in something or with someone. Sometimes you forget all about eating, and then remember to eat because you are suddenly hungry. That is why you can go through unusual weight and energy swings at differ-ent times of your life. This psychic sense is often associated with people who are absent-minded, simply because their thoughts are elsewhere. This distraction of thought means that you can, when extremely distracted, forget to eat completely, or suddenly eat two meals one straight after the other. This eating pattern can put your body under stress because it doesn't know whether to expect a feast or a famine. Sometimes you can put on weight because you tend not to have a balance to your eating patterns, and when you eat you may eat too much all in the one go!

Because psychic hearing is so close to thinking or talking to yourself, many people with this psychic gift think that they are just talking to themselves or 'echoing' their own thoughts back at themselves. Little do they know that if they asked a definite question, they are likely to receive an enlightened answer.

For these 'hearers' I recommend writing down actual questions you would like to ask your higher self. I do this when I want a specific answer to come to me. For example, this is what I do if

I have lost a book I was reading. I will ask my inner self to help me find the book and I will write it down as a request on a piece of paper—'please help me find that missing book'. Then I forget about it and just go about my normal business. Usually, before too long has passed, I come across the missing item, or a voice prompts me in the middle of the night to get up and look on the sideboard, (or somewhere else) and there that book is, just waiting for me to find it.

Many geniuses, particularly spiritual advisers, inventors and writers, have operated in this way. Einstein himself said he used to travel on a beam of light up to his soul, get his messages or insights, and then return to his body with the information he desired. I often have thought of Einstein (after reading this about him) as being a very attuned, highly receptive psychic hearer. It is interesting to note that Einstein was born under the very sensitive sign of Pisces. People I regard as possible psychic hearers include: Albert Einstein, David Letterman, Shirley MacLaine, Steven King, Deepak Chopra, Marianne Williamson and Barbara Walters.

Psychic Vision

Often termed 'visionaries', those who experience psychic vision, or clairvoyance, actually have visions or experiences pass in front of their eyes. Many of the best psychics have this ability where they can see a scene unfold before their eyes, as if watching a movie. Individuals with psychic vision, when trained and guided at will to tap into this psychic state, can look back into the past as well as project into the future. The part of the body associated with the state of psychic vision is the third eye area, located in the middle of the forehead. Most of us have experienced a state of psychic vision at some point in our lives. Every time you have a daydream you are, in a way, tapping into your sense of psychic vision.

Laziness is the big downfall for this sense when it comes to dieting as psychic visionaries often use cigarettes as their diet pills instead of eating wisely or monitoring their food intake. Their power to visualise can help them to lose weight rapidly if they set their minds to it; however, sometimes they just don't bother. Psychic visionaries love watching movies or television and enjoy eating while they do it. They are the kind of people who can sit and watch the grass grow. Those born with this psychic sense probably had the term 'couch potato' created just for them. Sitting around eating is often just fine with them, however, when committed to losing weight, they can lose it quite rapidly or efficiently. They do this by envisioning their new slim bodies and the fun they are going to have living in them. They are the type of person who sticks the slim and trim photo of themselves from years ago (or someone svelte, like Elle Macpherson), on their refrigerator to remind them of how they want to look. This group often spends a lot of their time in a somewhat distracted state of mind, but when they are focused they can be extremely creative. The psychic visionary can truly lose weight quickly if they learn to master the art of inner reflection, visual meditation or imagery (visualising and imagery exercises are covered in Chapter 8). Using their mind, or imaginings, to create their futures is usually part and parcel of their innate character. Because psychic visionaries have these talents operating in their lives, without being aware of it, they often seem to have the knack of being able to position themselves well in life. They also seem to have the capacity for being highly strung and a little irrational at times, and can be complex individuals. Possible clairvoyants include: Nicole

Kidman, Gwyneth Paltrow, Nicolas Cage, Bruce Willis, Robert de Niro, Julia Roberts, Michael Jackson, Sharon Stone, Tony Robbins and Cher.

Which Psychic Sense are You?

Some of you probably have some idea about whether or not you are tuned into your psychic senses. The following quiz will help you determine more specifically which psychic senses you are most attuned to. Answer yes or no to the following questions. The more 'yes' answers you have under a particular category, the more attuned you are to that sense.

Are You a Psychic Feeler?

1. When you enter a room, do you notice how the room FEELS to you? Is there a sense of feeling comfortable and at ease in that place, or not?
2. When you meet someone, regardless of their looks or behaviour, do you feel something very strongly about whether you are drawn to that person, or repelled by them?
3. When something dangerous is around you, do you sense it even before it has occurred or has become apparent?
4. If you make a decision about something, do you sometimes have a feeling about it—a very strong feeling, almost a fore-boding that you have made a mistake and you need to change your decision, otherwise your feelings will overwhelm you?
5. Can you only wear certain outfits, clothes or colours on certain days—days that the clothes 'feel right' to you?

6. If you are around people with problems or illnesses do you feel as if you are exchanging energy with them or becoming caught up in their lives or that they are draining you dry?

Are You a Psychic Intuitive?

1. Do you frequently 'know' the answers to things that it is impossible for you to know in advance?
2. Do you find yourself frequently in the right place at the right time?
3. Do your hunches often turn out to be very accurate and spot on?
4. Do you find it easy to make decisions?
5. Once you have a sense that you 'know' something, is it virtually impossible for anything, or anyone, else to alter your point of view? Are you sometimes called stubborn by those who know you well?
6. Do you often come out with insights or statements that shock other people because you are coming out with accurate information about them that nobody else knows?

Are You a Psychic Hearer?

1. Do you hear your name being called without it actually being spoken?
2. Do you often hear 'between the lines', as if you are tuning into dialogue from another person's thoughts that aren't actually being expressed outwardly?
3. Do you hear a song in your mind with words that actually provoke some insights or information that you are seeking?

4. Do you find yourself 'talking to yourself' but at the same time hearing echo-type answers coming back to you?
5. Do other people frequently say to you, 'Did you just say something?' when you have said absolutely nothing at all?
6. Have you ever been inspired into action by hearing your inner voice tell you something positive like, 'You can do it! Nothing can stop you' or perhaps giving you a warning like, 'Watch out' and providing you with information that you knew was accurate advice for you?

Are You a Psychic Visionary?

1. In a dream we see without using our eyes. Do you ever have dreams that have strong links with your reality at a particular time?
2. Do you ever walk into a room or a scene and have a sense of déjà vu, as if you had seen that place before at another time, even though you have never been there before?
3. Do you often have pictures flash through your mind that leave you with a strong impression—sometimes such powerful images that you never forget them?
4. Do you sometimes see an image of a friend or someone you know in your mind, and then they contact you either by person, phone or mail?
5. Have you ever pictured a scene in your mind where something goes wrong, only to find that at another time and place, you live out that scene in reality, or see it reenacted involving other people on the television?
6. Do you notice things in the world around you that are connected to other people, which are overlooked by most people?

How your Star Sign Fits into the Different Groups of Psychic Senses and Mind Power States

As a guideline only, here is the way the different star signs fall into the different psychic senses. Each individual can fine-tune their psychic development at any time and learn to focus on a specific area of their psychic unfoldment, thereby breaking out of their star sign's general psychic group. However, no matter what sign you are, knowingly or unknowingly, most people experience two of the four psychic senses, on either an advanced or subtle level, throughout different times of their lives.

The first psychic sense listed for each sign is usually the stronger one for them (the more highly developed).

Star Sign	Psychic Sense
Aries	psychic hearing, psychic intuition
Taurus	psychic vision, psychic feeling
Gemini	psychic intuition, psychic hearing
Cancer	psychic feeling, psychic intuition
Leo	psychic hearing, psychic intuition
Virgo	psychic vision, psychic feeling
Libra	psychic intuition, psychic hearing
Scorpio	psychic feeling, psychic intuition
Sagittarius	psychic hearing, psychic intuition.
Capricorn	psychic vision, psychic feeling
Aquarius	psychic intuition, psychic hearing
Pisces	psychic feeling, psychic intuition.

Chapter Four
Practical and Easy Psychic Tests for Everyone

Everybody is psychic, but we all have our good or bad psychic days. Athena

Following are some immediate tests to do to discover your psychic inclinations. The idea behind experimenting with psychic tests is to get your mind working in a new way. If you want to start running your life, instead of your life running you, you need to relearn how to use your mind in a powerful, unique and focused fashion. Simple fun things like experimenting with psychic tests will help you tune into your own mental powers and, once you can do this, you can use this power to stop eating so much food or doing the things you dislike.

Consider honing your mind-focusing energy (and doing psychic tests) as like learning to drive a car. Instead of becoming used to pushing the different pedals of the car around or moving the indicators, you are learning to 'drive around in your mind'. With practice, you can start to go in the direction that you want to travel—in your life. What a fantastic feeling that is! How satisfying to see yourself walk away from food or other temptations simply because your mind is strong enough now to say 'no' to temptation.

It is also important to realise that our psychic abilities are not constant—they alter all the time and go up and down somewhat, just as our moods change in everyday life. You may discover that there will be certain times of the day, week or month (such as a full moon or a new moon), when you may be more psychic. Psychic vision cannot be forced; it has to flow naturally. You may have one day where you may not be able to tap into your psychic self at all. As a guideline, many professional psychics believe that they sense things easier after a meal, which tends to ground them. Others work best in the early morning or late at night. Therefore, there are definite fluctuations in accessing your psychic higher self. The same occurs when you visit a professional psychic. You may get them on a good or bad psychic day.

Because psychic ability comes from raising the intuitive sense from the lower mind level to the more inspirationally based higher mind level (from the earthbound level to the more spirit or heaven attuned level), it is important that prior to doing your psychic test, you put your mind into a peaceful, more spiritual, type of place. Find yourself a quiet and comfortable place, away from any interruption. For example, unless you are very focused and disciplined, it is not wise to psychically test yourself with a television or radio blasting away in the background, because just when your soul or spirit is about to move and speak through you, something may happen on the television or radio which pulls your attention towards it and breaks the connection you are forging with your higher self.

Before commencing these tests it is wise to set and promote a scene that is conducive to creating a psychic sensory atmosphere. Below are some easy tests that will reveal how developed your psychic abilities are. You will need:

One dice (a single dice is correctly called a 'die' but I will use the word 'dice' instead because it is harmonious to the unconscious senses, even if grammatically incorrect)

One deck of playing cards (preferably new)

Five different coloured jellybeans or Smarties

One small brown paper bag

Before commencing any psychic test, have a piece of paper and a pencil ready and find yourself a comfortable location. When you are settled, close your eyes and say inwardly to yourself: 'I reach up to you, my psychic higher self. Will you guide me today?' Repeat this several times and say it with sincerity and deep-felt feeling. Then when you feel relaxed and your mind is clear of any self-talk or chatter, commence the first psychic test. Be sure when doing the first test, and the one after that, that you remain in this peaceful, focused, noise-free frame of mind. This may mean that you need to pause between tests and commence the process all over again, particularly if there are interruptions of any kind or there is a lot of outside noise or distraction going on around you.

The Dice Test

This test will tune you into your ability to tap into and sense the vibrational frequency (or harmonics) surrounding different numbers.

Take the single dice in your hands and roll it around in both palms, putting your energy into it and letting its energy merge into your own (so that you and the dice become one).

Attempt to see in your mind's eye the number that is going to appear when you roll the dice. You should actually see a picture of it or hear the number spoken in your mind.

It isn't wise to strain or force yourself, so relax and simply let the number appear before you, rather than pushing your energy in an attempt to make it come to you in your mind. Don't focus on seeing a number on its own, either. Instead, expect to see the dice with a number between one and six showing on it. Concentrate on any messages you are receiving from the dice.

On the piece of paper you have with you, write down the number when you 'feel' or 'sense' it. Now actually throw the dice and note down the number that comes up. Whether you are right or wrong, write down the number that appears next to your 'envisioned' number. Repeat this process nine times, then tally up how many times you sensed the die's number or guessed correctly.

SCORING:
0–2 is average
3–5 means you are tapping into your psychic ability, but hold some self-doubts about it and are pushing the messages away
6–9 means you already have highly developed psychic abilities

The Playing Card Test

This test will see how well you can sense the patterns or pictures that are about to be presented to you. Ideally a new pack of cards should be used, because otherwise there could be unusual energy coming from the cards which mislead your psychic reading. Handling the cards is most important as it imprints them with your personal vibrations. However, if a new pack isn't available, you should shuffle and cut and handle the used cards for at least five minutes before using them—that way you can rid them of any previous influences.

For this test you will need twenty cards—any five cards from each suit (hearts, clubs, spades and diamonds). Shuffle these cards well and be sure you look at their pictures during the five-minute shuffle to get their images in your mind.

Once you are ready to do your psychic test, turn the cards face-down and shuffle them again for another minute or so. Then concentrate upon the top card. Touch this card and guess whether it is a heart, club, spade or diamond. In your imagination or mind's eye, see yourself turning this card over and what you will see when you do. Write down whatever your mind tells you the suit is. Then turn the card over and make a note of the actual suit of the card. Reshuffle the cards again and repeat this test for a total of eighteen times.

SCORING:
0–5 average
6–11 some psychic ability
12–18 highly developed psychic ability

The Colour Test

For this test you will need five jellybeans (or Smarties) of different colours. You will also need a small brown paper bag to put them in.

Before commencing this test, hold the jellybeans in your hands and try to merge with their energies, moving and shaking them between your palms. When you feel that your energy has gone into the jellybeans, and their energy has gone into you, place them in the paper bag and shake them around again.

Next reach into the bag and select one jellybean, but do not remove it from the bag so that you can see it. While holding the jellybean, concentrate. Attempt to visualise what colour this bean is with your mind's divine eye. Imagine yourself pulling the bean out of the bag and the colour it will be when you do. When you have got a feeling for the colour of the jellybean, write it down, then pull the jellybean out of the bag and record its actual colour. Repeat this test nine times.

SCORING:
0–2 average
3–5 some psychic ability
6–9 highly developed psychic ability

Chapter Five
The Psychic Flow Chart

You can quickly develop and utilise your own psychic powers.
Athena

In this chapter you will enter the realm of psychic exploration and how you can exchange psychic mental energy with me. The psychic energy realignment and body realignment flow chart on page 49 will connect you to my psychic and mental capabilities. The flow chart provides the visual images and means to practise, not only psychic energy attunement with the help of me, but also the ability to focus on and develop your own psychic powers.

To begin, put the middle finger of your right hand (if you are right-handed), or the middle finger of your left hand (if you are left-handed), on the area of the body you want to affect, change or improve in any way, shape or form.

You can use this chart to reshape your body, remove stress from that area of the body, or to help you place a special focus of psychic energy on certain parts of the body. Singling out a part of your body can help you revitalise and heal yourself in that particular area. It gives you added power in this area of the body.

In the psychic energy realignment and re-balancing flow chart, every main energy centre (the energy centre points in some cultures are called chakras) is marked with a circle. By placing your middle finger on the circle that is situated close to the part of the body you wish to influence, you can really use your psychic powers with force. As well as psychically re-balancing and re-attuning various parts of the body and to assist with weight loss, placing your finger anywhere on the chart will help you release any emotional blocks or tension in those specific areas of your body. It provides a form of psychic healing and magic massage.

Once again by touching the chart on the area which denotes or represents the part of your body where any stress, pain, tension or an emotional block is felt, this creates a subliminal psychic energy flow (an invisible electric psychic magnetic field). Touching the chart returns the energy flow of the individual to a more relaxed, flowing state. When you master the art of psychic realignment and re-attunement you are not only helping yourself, but also those around you.

Just by stopping and taking the time to touch the psychic flow chart (and by focusing on certain body parts and also thinking of me), you are undertaking a very powerful mental action. This is a giant step forward in your own mind's attunement. This flow chart will assist you in resetting your mind's attention and reorganising your focus on altering your body shape and achieving your personal goals. This one simple action and mental procedure is an extremely powerful one. It can assist you in overcoming any destructive personality traits that previously encouraged you to succumb to weakness.

When you look at the body flow chart, you'll also see that there are certain colours indicated on various parts of the body (they flow through from the front to the back of your body). These are provided to help you go one step further into the energy flow process of the body—if you would like to expand upon your experience. If you want to include the colours when you use the body energy flow chart—and have a certain body area for your mental target—before you put your mind to work, think of or picture the colour that is shown on the body flow chart for that specific body area (or envision that colour in your mind). When you do this, it will help your thought power process to work more powerfully. However, if you find this attention to colour detail too difficult or confusing, just ignore this part of the exercise, and keep your focus on the body part only.

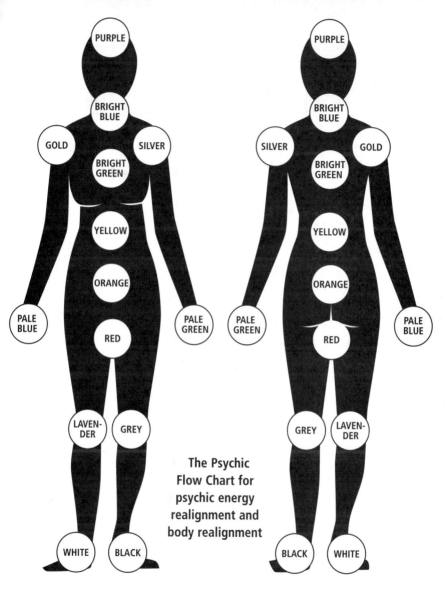

The Psychic Flow Chart for psychic energy realignment and body realignment

Chapter Six
Start Mastering Your Life to Reclaim Your Lost Personal Power!

Bathroom scales are not magic. They are often mean, nasty, horrible things! Athena

Now it is time for you to begin to change your life around for the better by doing things differently and thinking different thoughts. To start your magic and psychic powers flowing in the right direction in order to upgrade your life, lose weight, love yourself and become the perfect shape, is to immediately *stop weighing yourself on the bathroom scales!*

In fact, I recommend you remove these scales from your home altogether. When you are overweight, checking how much you weigh on the scales only reinforces the fact that you are unhappy and overweight. Bathroom scales can have you tuning your mind into the opposite realm of magic—the realm of depressed and negative thoughts. For many people, seeing their bathroom scales, reminds them of all the things they are unhappy about.

At your weakest and most vulnerable moments—the times when you really need support, love and encouragement—

your bathroom scales can become the cause of tremendous grief, guilt and anxiety.

Here is my approach to reclaiming my personal power, and I think it is marvellous for gaining control over your weight. I do not weigh myself and I do not know how much I weigh. I don't think about weight or how much I weigh. Instead I affirm to myself:

I am just me.
I do not focus on my weight.
I just see myself as slim and beautiful.

Mind power studies have shown that the more a person thinks they are overweight, the more overweight they are likely to become. Putting on weight is fuelled by our thoughts, particularly if the things we are thinking about are food or our next meal! Also dwelling on the fact that we feel overweight and do not like ourselves does not help. This type of negative thought focus means *disaster is imminent!*

Smart People Eat Moderately —So Get Smart!

The instant you start to take control of your life by practising your psychic and mental powers, you will become more powerful and physically attuned to your mind and body. It is also likely that you will suddenly discover that you can, more or less, eat whatever you want without regaining weight!

How does this happen that you can eat without adding weight? It is to do with your mind changing the metabolic rhythm of your body. Once you change your mind's outlook, you become a different person than the one you were before. You begin to operate differently from the old you. Consequently, you will no longer have an appetite for the things you used to eat. Your appetite or your desire for certain foods will have altered and shifted.

This means that when you start using your mind differently, you are not just changing or reshaping your appetite or your body shape, but also your destiny. When you are more powerfully attuned psychically, what you eat doesn't affect you like it did previously. Your appetite no longer influences how you put on weight or stay slim and trim. You stabilise. Now food keeps you energised and vital. This is because when you are in the mental, psychic and physical flow, your body happily deals with whatever you eat. You will probably find that eating moderately becomes second nature to you now.

My Ideal Diet

Because I am slim, people often ask me what I eat, but the surprising thing is that, in reality, *I eat a lot for a slim person*. In fact, some people think I am far too skinny. I believe I stay so skinny, without gaining weight, because I am psychically attuned and I think before I eat. I am not perfect. I have my good days and bad days like everyone else. Like most people, my life takes me through all kinds of patterns and circumstances. There are times when I eat something I wish I had not eaten. I'll eat a whole tub of frozen yoghurt in one overly indulgent sitting, but most times I am totally health conscious.

Below is a list of what I have found to be my ideal diet through much exploration and experience. In order to find the right diet for you, you have to experiment with different foods to ascertain what suits your individual energy needs. Remember with food that 'less is best'. A light diet is uplifting and energising. A heavy diet is tiring and draining. Eating light healthy meals have been shown to increase longevity, provide more physical energy and sharpen the mind. Once you start eating well, you'll notice an enormous difference to your entire physical feeling and mental energy levels (like improved concentration). Shifting over from one diet to another (especially if you've been pigging out on fries, soft drinks, ice-cream and chocolate) can be initially tough. You get cravings for these food stuffs because they are laced with additives or other horrid ingredients that get into your system and make you almost addicted to them. You'll need to go through an initial period of cleansing to get rid of these cravings—a period of eating no sugar or foods high in fat—so the longing for these foods goes out of your physical system. When you have cravings for sweet or fattening food, that's where the photograph of me and the psychic energy flow chart in this book can help. Use the photo of me to take you through the first few days of sugar withdrawals. Look into my eyes and think healthy thoughts. Remind yourself to eat wisely and to strengthen your willpower. You can also use the flow chart to help alleviate any cravings. Single out the part of your body that you want to revitalise and unblock any tension you may feel in this area.

Once you've passed that initial 'craving' period, you'll discover that eating healthy food is not just enjoyable, it is energising and builds your self-confidence. What follows is the food program I follow (with some modifications) on a day-to-day basis:

Breakfast

Half a rockmelon (cantaloupe) with cottage cheese. One croissant or two slices of wholegrain toast with slices of grilled tomato on top, or, as a treat, a little jam. (I'm not perfect—I know I shouldn't have butter or jam, but I do!) One glass of water. One or two cups of very weak decaffeinated tea or coffee with a dash of milk. (I usually have decaffeinated coffee or tea once a day and this is with my breakfast.)

Lunch

Chicken soup or salad (or sometimes both if I am really hungry), or sushi. I am a big sushi eater. I have no oil on the salad, just some Balsamic vinegar. I really love the taste of Balsamic vinegar on salad. I seem to have a bad physical reaction to oils, so I always ask for no oil in my meals when I eat out.

Dinner

Soup, salad or steamed asparagus to start. A small serving of grilled chicken or fish with vegetables (again no butter or oil on the chicken or fish). I also love to eat steak every now and again (a leftover taste desire from my Australian meat-eating heritage I guess, because as a child, my mother prepared many meat dishes for our meals so I got accustomed to eating meat).

However, the main trick for me remaining slim, trim and feeling terrific is NO ALCOHOL (or very little of it, say just a small glass of wine for a celebratory occasion). I am lucky with alcohol, because if I drink alcohol, I pay a huge price for it almost immediately. I lose my mental awareness and willpower very quickly and usually regret it. Alcohol tends to sap my energy away. So the universe has made sure I can't become an 'everyday' drinker— I would spend most of my life in bed recovering if I tried to do that! I feel blessed that this is the case and my body rejects alcohol.

Although alcohol may be a tough thing to give up for some of you, if you really wish to have control of your mind—and therefore run your own life—it is important not to drink any alcohol!

I think anyone who is psychically sensitive probably suffers similar bad side effects from drinking alcohol. This substance certainly isn't good for anyone who is trying to strengthen their willpower or trying to be creatively in control of their existence, because alcohol shifts your mind around, weakens your resolve, and dilutes your psychic and mental powers.

Banish Sweet Cravings!

What a shame sweets are just literally the devil's food. So many people find themselves tormented when it comes to sugar cravings. However, when it comes to staying slim and trim, sweets are definitely a sure way of sabotaging your prospects. Losing weight is tough if you always have your hand in the cookie jar. However, sweets often are simply substitutes for what you really want or are not getting enough of, such as love, sex, affection, or attention. To be psychically powerful, you have to be self-sufficient and tune into your higher being to receive the love and affection you crave from the food of life (rather than food stuffs) around you. Fill yourself up on a sunset, or with children's laughter. Get divinely intoxicated by listening to incredible music. Smell a flower. Sit and think about all the things and people you have in your life and be grateful for them. These kinds of higher-level thoughts can replace any food temptations because as it has been said, 'things of the physical senses, never truly satisfy the soul'. It is food for the heart that satisfies the soul.

If you can connect with your higher love, you'll be amazed at how your sweet cravings will disappear! A chunk of higher love is far better for you on all levels of your existence than, say, a big chunk of chocolate.

When tempted, no matter how much you want that pancake with syrup, the hamburger with fries, or the chocolate fudge sundae, you must say to yourself:

I know it is not good for me.
I know it will make me feel worse later, and I won't feel good about myself.

So, if you must have dessert, I would recommend something like sorbet or fruit. Fruit has become my preferred dessert and I make sure I buy luscious, healthy, vibrant fresh fruit to satisfy my sugar cravings.

Often I do feel like eating sweets or ice-cream (yes, I get that crazy desire to munch on all the bad stuff too!), but when I am really in tune and don't succumb to temptation, I try to take some time out to reflect upon what is happening in my life. I have noticed that the times I feel like eating desserts are often when I have had several late nights in a row, I feel overtired, or I am worried about something.

When you are experiencing ho-hum doldrum states of mind, eating sugar is actually the worst thing you can do. Once the sugar has taken you through the momentary pleasure stage, it tires you out even more. Instead of eating sweets, I make a conscious effort to do some exercise, make a phone call or keep busy doing whatever else I can think of, in order to shift my thoughts away from sweet-eating temptation...and towards inspiration instead. Usually when I do these little mind tricks, I no longer want anything sweet! The feeling has passed. Try it, it works!

The great thing is that once you get your mind's psychic powers flowing, filling up on sweets, desserts or cookies will not be so attractive anymore.

I have found that when I am psychically powerful, my emotional instabilities are gone, and when this occurs, my sugar cravings disappear. That is when my mind is attuned to its higher powers and my unsettled emotions or moods are no longer running my life. Therefore the desire or craving for sweet things dissipates or disappears. So if you are greatly tempted by desserts, use your own psychic powers to settle you inwardly and help you temper your sweet tooth.

Chapter Seven
Recognise Your Perfect Weight Enemies

Don't indulge in too much food, wine and desserts! These indulgences become our body, mind and spirit's worst enemies.

Athena

When you decide to become your perfect weight and develop your innermost psychic flow and willpower, it can be very helpful if you *view yourself as going to war*—a war of wills against your renegade weaker self. To begin to master your life and reclaim your perfect weight is really no game, it is, in fact, the real secret of living a fulfilling and successful life.

Reclaiming your power begins with recognising the enemy or enemies that keep you from living your true potential. However, recognising your real enemies may not come easily. Your enemies are likely to appear in a very socially acceptable and cleverly disguised innocent form (like the nibblies that surround you when you attend your local sewing group, or the local residents' association, where hot chocolate with marshmallows is always the tempting drink of the evening. It may even be your Auntie Denise's famous pavlova, which is always something that cries out for you to have seconds, covered with lashings of fresh cream).

When you are attempting to lose weight, visiting certain locations, relatives, associates or restaurants suddenly begins to test your will. Your enemy may be something as easily seductive as the chocolate bar you buy when you visit your local video store, or as rich as the butter you plaster all over that breakfast bagel every day. Your enemy may be a simple as the teaspoon of sugar you add to your coffee, the glass of wine you have with dinner, the scoop of ice-cream you accompany tinned fruit, or drinks such as Coca Cola that become an accepted and regular part of your everyday diet. These enemies are the ones you use without thinking of the consequences. Yet, whatever the form this temptation or indulgence takes, behind its tasty and friendly veneer, it is truly your most dreaded enemy. However, as it is the enemy with a thousand faces, you probably don't even think about it as a foe. Until you recognise these small additions to your food as detrimental to your weight loss, you might instead, misguidedly and innocently, consider them as friends. You may even perceive them as your great pleasure, when in truth they are the source of your heartache, unhappiness and innermost pain. And because you don't even consider these additions as your likely enemies, unwittingly you will eat them...without even realising the negative effect they are having on your health and that they are not only conquering you but also prosper and grow in power over you—at YOUR EXPENSE!

Write down a list of your enemies and from this day forth decide you are going to defeat them. They will never, ever conquer or fool you again!

Enemy No. 1 ....
Enemy No. 2 ....

Enemy No. 3 ....
Enemy No. 4 ....
Enemy No. 5 ....
Enemy No. 6 ....
Enemy No. 7 ....
Enemy No. 8 ....
Enemy No. 9 ....
Enemy No. 10 ....

Once you realise who and what are your enemies, you will become aware of the things that are stopping you from living the life of your dreams, loving yourself or being happier with your life. When you are armed with this enlightening knowledge, you have a target to go after because you realise which enemies you need to eradicate from your life. By listing your enemies you acknowledge where some of your problems are stemming from. Once you define your enemies and appreciate how much unhappiness those items, foods or pastimes are creating for you, then you can launch your attack on them and rid them from your life—once and for all!

Chapter Eight
See Yourself as Thin and Beautiful by Using Self-imagery

To see yourself in the mirror as beautiful is the first step in becoming that way. Beauty always has been, and always will be, in the eye of the beholder. Athena

By the time you have reached this chapter you have probably come to grips with the fact that you have certain tendencies or habits in life that could be improved, and certain food preferences you need to put aside. If you are using the psychic and mental weight loss program, by now you should have experienced my psychic support through the psychically energised photo attached to this book. You can strategically place copies of this photo in your home or office to ensure you remain psychically and mentally aware and practise constant willpower.

In this chapter, you are now entering into the next phase of your psychic and mental journey, where you personally, through your own wilful thoughts, commence to remould, reshape and redesign your 'self' on many levels through the use of self-imagery and magic energies (your own mind and psychic focused powers).

Let me tell you more about self-imagery and imagery because it is one of the most valuable psychic and mental tools or accomplishments you can ever have at your disposal. I have used imagery, magic energies and self-imagery for many years with great success.

How Imagery Has Worked For Me

I owe a tremendous amount of the true joy in my life to imagery and self-imagery. Imagery is making things in general happen; while self-imagery is improving your outlook or appearance by the mental picture you have of yourself.

I use imagery to stay at what I feel is the perfect weight for me; to keep myself fit; and to help me get the jobs that I want. I also use imagery to 'create' the circumstances or opportunities that I desire to have happen around me. For example, it was through using imagery that I became the proud owner of my house at Whale Beach in Sydney, Australia, back in 1981. At the time I had no intention of buying a house, but it kind of just happened—as if by magic. Incredibly, I knew that I wanted a house, but before I even began to think about buying one realistically, I actually 'saw' the house in my mind in detail (not that I had ever seen the house before, it was the house of my imaginings!). I saw myself living in the house, walking down its driveway, taking a shower, collecting my mail from the mailbox. Moreover, after having that vision of myself living there, the way the events fell into place to buy that house was astounding. I believe I got that house through using imagery, because there is no other logical explanation for the events that unfolded mentally. It was as though fate and fortune worked together to ensure that house became mine.

After I saw my vision of the house I wanted to live in, the house I was then renting in Whale Beach started falling down around my ears—literally! It was an old house ready for the bulldozer. Therefore, fate forced me to go out and find another house to rent, or to buy. The latter naturally appealed to my Cancer home-making spirit, however, the problem was that I had no money! Houses at Whale Beach (a gorgeous peninsular in the northern beaches district of Sydney), are at the high end of the real estate market. However, I kept my creative imagery going and continued to see myself as the proud owner of the house. It was a unique house, because it had a long driveway and a parking area for several cars—both these qualities are unusual for the area. My imagery kept giving me a message that the house was 'beautiful'. When I telephoned the realtor and told her I was after a house to purchase, I could have fallen over when she told me she had a bargain available—my heart skipped a beat! Moreover, to my advantage, the owners were in a serious financial bind and were desperate to sell.

From that moment, like magic, all the things I needed to buy the house fell into place. The people who were selling it were fantastically helpful; they lowered the price even more and gave me time to conjure up the money to buy it. I was able to come up with the deposit through getting myself a credit card with every bank in town and taking out cash deposits on each one! Then, a bank loaned me the remaining balance at a very low interest rate. Within six weeks, I had the house. As soon as I moved in to my new home, I attracted a whole lot of new work. This meant that I ended up paying that house off totally in three years. I have used creative imagery ever since, because I know how powerfully the forces of fate can work for you when you project your mind outwards to fulfill a goal or a dream.

Apart from my house buying, which was my first real imagery success, for the past fifteen years, I have also used self-imagery successfully to keep myself young. I have used it to reshape my body form, to lengthen and thicken my hair, to make myself taller, to connect with my true love, to go on dream holidays, to get my life going in New York, and no end of other wondrous things. You can do all these things, and more, for yourself too, anytime and anywhere.

I am not alone in using imagery. It has been used in most cultures, for good and, naturally, sometimes for mischief too! Just as electricity, knives, water, ropes and fire can be used for good and bad, imagery is a strong force or implement that must be used with the right intention. Shaman, witchdoctors, holy men and Australian Aboriginal medicine men use imagery to empower themselves and to make life's progress move in the direction they desire. Imagery provided a powerful means to heal and, if the occasion called for it, wreak punishment!

Australian Aborigines, as an example, used to perform a rather wicked ceremony called 'pointing the bone'. They would 'point the bone' if they wanted to seek revenge on someone who had broken the rules or taboos of their tribe. This was a ceremony where the tribal elders sat around and chanted in order to work up their collective psychic powers. At the high point of the ceremony, all kinds of strange animal bones were released from a special bag and then cast into the middle of the tribal elders' magic circle. When the bones were cast from the bag, this was when the ceremony took effect. The person to whom these elders were 'pointing the bone', who may have been located hundreds of miles away, would get knocked over by the force of pointing the bone during this ceremony. Sometimes they were knocked over with such force that they came to a rather uncomfortable end. Naturally, this is a form of imagery that is used in a destructive way, but it reveals how powerful collective minds can be when used for positive or negative results.

Our mind, both individually and collectively, can play a huge role in creating illnesses too. For example, were you aware that when a new illness, like a new form of a cold virus, is announced in the newspapers and the illness' symptoms are described, people all over the country suddenly come down with it? Whether people have the illness or not, when they know about it, their mind is strong enough to create the symptoms in their own body (like the phantom pregnancy syndrome mentioned in an earlier chapter).

Our minds are also impacted by something we read about in the newspapers, see on the television or hear about on the radio. The input our minds receive can affect us very strongly. What we hear about, read about or see on television can influence our own lives, even if it is to our disadvantage to do so. We can be run by our own imagery, and when our imagery is uncontrolled or not recognised or understood, usually it works against us.

While it may be a bitter pill to swallow at times, the harsh truth is that, through our mind's deep-seated imagery and beliefs, we unconsciously play a major role in attracting events or situations upon ourselves.

Our society practises imagery in many ways. You will see it consciously practised through meditation groups, through various art forms and subconsciously when people listen to music or the radio. The radio, in particular, is a very profound and specific 'imagery creator'. Without being instructed to do so, the listener is encouraged to listen to the words or messages they hear on the radio and from this input, conjure up their own mental images of what is taking place.

This makes me remember a particularly hilarious radio show in Australia years ago, which featured Grahame Bond, who achieved great notoriety when he portrayed 'Auntie Jack', and who, at one time, had his own radio show. On this radio show, which was called 'Nude Radio', Grahame and all his guests were supposed to be doing the show in the nude. Just the 'image' of this was so ridiculous and funny, that the show automatically created a controversy. Whether they were indeed sitting around nude (which I doubt!) or not, just imagining them sitting in the studio with the funny suggestions and asides they made about their nudity, made it seem like they were naked. That is the way 'imagery' works. It is theatre of the mind.

Even television, which, unlike radio, has its vision pictures or images, still gives the viewer a chance to come up with their own form of interpretation or co-imagery. Studies on television show audiences reveal that no two people who view the same television program see what is occurring on the screen in exactly the same way. Each interprets what they see within the boundaries of their own belief systems, experience and preferences.

Psychotherapists use imagery or guided focus of the mind as a form of centering, strengthening, relaxing and many other forms of psychological attunement in their consultations with patients. Imagery practices, particularly in athletics, which is covered later in this chapter, have been developed to promote particular virtues, skill and capacities.

Self-imagery is known by many names, such as 'creative visualisation', 'directed daydreaming', 'dream drama', and 'mental imagery'. For the purposes of this book, the self-imagery I am going to teach you is designed to empower and strengthen your willpower. Self-imagery will assist you to lose weight and to get the things happening in your life that you want to happen, such as finding true love, developing a more happy-go-lucky nature, and even improving your finances too.

Don't misguidedly think that 'self-imagery' is anything new to you or the world at large...every single person is 'self-creating' all the time! The difference is that once you start to practise 'self-imagery', you are doing it now with focus, intention and direction and targeting it specifically to areas of your life that you want to upgrade and improve upon.

Self-imagery is part and parcel of our everyday existence. For example, just thinking of yourself and seeing yourself in the mirror as overweight is a form of self-imagery. Every time you look in the mirror and tell yourself, 'I am fat,' confirms and affirms that state to every part of your mind and body. You end up creating the very thing you don't want—a negative self-image (similar to every time you step onto the bathroom scales and they give you the bad news about your weight!)

When you practise my form of self-imagery, you focus on what you want to happen in your life in your inner-mind's eye, through a form of intense imagining.

The secret to the success with self-imagery is that when you do it, you see what you want as already being accomplished. You don't see yourself becoming slim—you are already slim.

To give you a sense of what I mean, imagine for a moment that you are an athlete using imagery to win the gold medal for the

Olympic marathon event. What you need to do is find a comfortable place to sit quietly, close your eyes and envisage yourself not as running the race, competing in the event, or even training for the event, but how you would *feel* when the event was completed and you are standing on the winner's podium as a gold medal Olympic winner.

The more vividly you can conjure up the vision and feel the sensation and experience of winning in that moment in time and space, the more the vibration of being a winner is flowing through you. You will create around you the frequency and dynamic energy (on the psychic levels of receptivity), of being a winner.

You can enhance the imagery experience by imagining your loved ones running up to you, thrilled with your win. It is imperative to attempt to not only envisage the scene in your mind, but to use all the senses including the auditory and olfactory. For example, imagine the cheers of the crowd all calling out your name. Expand your inner awareness so that you can visualise every single detail of the feeling after the event, in as fine detail as possible, even to the point of smelling the scent in the air at that moment.

Now you should have some idea of what I am trying to pass over to you and you can start your own self-imagery exercise.

Starting Your Own Imagery

I recommend that you start your very first self-imagery exercise with a twenty-minute session, imaging yourself as slim, trim and terrific. You can make it five minutes or ten minutes in length, but I have found that twenty minutes works best for me. Be sure that when you do your imagery, you position yourself somewhere quiet and take the telephone off the hook. Do not leave the television or radio on as they will only distract you. Start your imagery at any time of the day that suits your own personal program. However, do not try to do your imagery lying down, because if you do, the pleasantness of the imagery may make you fall asleep. The ideal position is to sit comfortably with your eyes closed. You must feel comfortable, because there should be no stress involved in this exercise. You are simply directing your mind into a space where you will feel good about yourself. In this first session, do nothing else but luxuriate in a vision or image of yourself where you are divinely slim and gorgeous.

During this imagery session, as well as seeing yourself looking great, imagine all the wonderful outfits you can wear now, including swimsuits. Visualise all the social benefits that will come your way as a natural course of things, because of your slimness. See how looking like this and feeling so fantastic enhances the romantic, social, financial, sexual, familial, professional, health, and spiritual aspects of your life. Go right into the imagery. Feel the way your new thin clothes fit on your body. Sense the way the clothes flow in the breeze, how people look at you, how light your step feels, and how gracefully you now move. Imagine how everyone will treat you. Strange men will hold doors open for you. Waiters will linger over you trying to help. Your husband or wife will take to massaging your feet (without you needing to ask). Passers-by will turn their heads on the street, to watch you walk by.

Align your slimness with every area of your existence. See how being slim and gorgeous will serve you. Imagine with all your psychic and higher senses how happy and fulfilled you are to be slim, proud, and in command of your body.

Do this imagery exercise at least once a day and while you are doing it, enjoy every single instant of it. It is your quality time— the time you give to yourself to invest your mind's thoughts on you. The moment you start to use imagery in a creative way you are starting to master your life. Imagery is no foolish time-wasting game to play. I believe our entire lives are run by imagery, particularly in our media-driven society.

Think Yourself Thin

When you use your mind's power to become your perfect weight, you need to be constantly watchful over what you are thinking, because your thoughts hold the power to success. Combined with self-imagery, affirmations (sentences or phrases that you repeat over and over to yourself in a disciplined and programmed manner), which are sometimes also called words of power, are effective mind tools that can assist you in gaining mastery over your life—and over your own destructive, random thoughts. What is so terrific about affirmations, is that you can say or think them anywhere—and they can be great time-fillers when you have to wait for something or someone.

There is no such thing as wasted time when you get into the habit of using words of power or affirmations. Those long queues you experience at the movies, the bank or the supermarket, suddenly take on a new value to your life. They become opportunities to say your affirmations. I seldom stand in line without remembering to do my words of power. In fact standing in line *reminds* me to do my affirmations. I also have a habit of doing my words of power when I am showering.

I have discovered that it is best to get into the habit of practising your mind power or psychic abilities, otherwise everyday life and responsibilities can distract you away from them. It is wise to allot yourself certain conditions, such as standing in a line or showering, or other times in your everyday flow, to do these exercises. When you get the psychic and mental ball rolling, then doing psychic or mind power exercises come automatically and naturally to you. And don't let your mind get the best of you. There are certain times when the only solution is to do affirmations or words of power. For example, any time when you find yourself entertaining doubts or negative thoughts, that is exactly when you want to take command of your own mind and thoughts and perform affirmations. Instead of fuelling and placing focus on panic or problems, redirect your mind into more positive directions by reciting (with heartfelt meaning), either aloud (if in private and it feels good to hear yourself), or within your own mind, your own special words of power or affirmations. I have also recorded mine to play to myself at night or when I am driving alone.

Remember to use your affirmations or words of power at any opportunity. As mentioned earlier, if you are waiting in the supermarket line or standing for the elevator at work; instead of just getting frustrated and feeling as if you are wasting time, utilise this time wisely by focusing on your words of power.

The utilisation of words of power seems easy because it is relatively effortless, but their true worth and potential should never be underestimated. A message repeated over and over soon becomes reality because our minds truly are the most magnificent creators. Never discredit the value of using words of power regularly, as they will become a constant in your mind.

Following are the affirmations that I use regularly, but it is wise to devise your own (which are likely to be similar to mine anyway), because you need to have an emotional connection with the words you use, so they are your own words, or have some kind of personal attachment to you.

Some of my affirmations include:
- I am the perfect weight, height and shape
- I love the way I look
- I am beautiful
- I am slim, tall and elegant
- I love myself and I am proud of the way I look
- I have unlimited willpower
- I love life and can't wait to jump out of bed every morning
- There are no problems, only opportunities.
- I have excellent health
- I love to eat nourishing, healthy food
- I love to exercise
- I love to look at myself in the mirror...nude!

Now that you have the general idea, you can use any of my affirmations (or none, if you wish), to create your own special affirmations. Words of power will help you to be an inspiration and guiding light to everyone around you. And remember, always say your affirmation in the present tense, as if it is already true.

Chapter Nine
Imagery Works Because What We Think About, We Bring About

When you see yourself as slim in your own mind, you are subliminally sending out signals to your cells and molecules to start working hard to make you slim. Athena

The question has often been posed: Does life imitate Hollywood or does Hollywood imitate life? If you understand the powers of self-imagery, you would tend to think that 'Life imitates Hollywood'. Hollywood projects and creates trends, fashionable body shapes, lifestyles, romances and violence through its movies. All these 'Hollywood conditions' get picked up and copied by the viewing public—even the horrible ones.

Now the point to this is, what you see in your mind is going to impact on you too (like Hollywood affects the movie-going public). So, why put a message or vision into your mind that isn't serving you well, or won't bring you any benefits? To see yourself as a person with a BFA (Big Fat Ass) will not help or serve you or anyone else. So if your current self-image mission is to lose weight, don't just envisage yourself as thin only when you do your self-imaging sessions. Begin to see yourself as slim and gorgeous when you look at yourself in the mirror. If you are overweight, seeing yourself as slim and trim when you aren't may sound foolish, but in fact, it is important to start believing that you are slim and gorgeous, no matter how you look right now. Once you start believing you are trim, you are sending yourself (mentally, emotionally and physically) a 'slim message'. By imagining yourself as slim, you are subliminally sending out signals to your cells and molecules to starting working hard to make you slim. When you see yourself as 'overweight' and feel unhappy and upset by what you see in the mirror, you are confirming to your body that you are over-weight and it keeps itself that way.

Even when you have those little 'self-talks' with yourself, when you yell at yourself or tell yourself, 'I am fat or overweight', it ensures that you stay that way. Why? This type of self-talk affirms that you are overweight to yourself. Through self-imagery you can begin to become slim and trim and as beautiful as you want to be...and you truly are beautiful, even as you already are, but that doesn't mean that you can't improve upon your beauty. Following is a quotation by the choreo-grapher Martha Graham (who died in 1991, aged 97 years young). She was a wonderful, vital and inspiring individual who brought her creative dance performances to the world stage. Martha was very strong-willed and she created her life in very specific detail through her own form of creative imagery. When I am down on myself, I read this wonderful quote by Martha. It constantly reminds me of my remarkable place in the universe as an individual. Maybe it will help you do the same too.

There is a vitality, a life force, an energy, a quickening that is translated through you into action. And because THERE IS ONLY ONE OF YOU IN ALL TIME, this expression is unique. And if you block it, it will never exist through any other medium...and the world will not have it. It is not your business to determine how good it is, nor how valuable! Nor how it compares with other expressions. It is your business to keep it yours, clearly and directly. To keep the channel open.

As Martha states in her quote above, whether you are fat or thin, short or tall—whatever form your physique takes—your expression of life means that you are unique and special. That is the cosmic universal truth. After all, we are all an expression of the divine spark of the creation of life and therefore *we are all beautiful*. But the way we 'think' of ourselves makes the big difference between living the life of our dreams...or of our nightmares. Much depends upon us being confident or self-conscious...and all of us deserve to believe and acknowledge we are beautiful in our own special way. So set yourself a goal to spend at least twenty minutes a day doing self-imagery with your eyes comfortably and dreamily closed, somewhere you won't be disturbed. Spend this time in your own special inner-imaging world. Here your powers of creation can be given a chance to work. See yourself as improving whatever it is that you personally want to improve upon in yourself. There are no limits either—you can be extremely creative with self-imaging. However, I personally believe (but not all other practitioners of imagery do), that there is a need for some sense of real connection with the image you put into your consciousness about yourself—it is good to have some solid foundations. I feel, especially when beginning this practice, that to be an efficient imager or creator, it is important to begin with one specific part of the body that you would love to improve upon and to build from there.

Radical transformations can and have occurred with self-imaging on many different levels, but you shouldn't get stuck in the form the results of your imaging may assume. Self-imaging doesn't necessarily mean that the transformation will occur simply through the mind's control over the body. It can instead create conditions that will bring that 'image' to a reality—in other words the will to repackage yourself. For example, a girl who imagines herself with long blonde hair may become involved with using hairpieces to enhance her appearance. Therefore, her own hair may remain the same colour, but through being introduced to the magic of hairpieces, she still has created the image she imagined herself to have. Or, she may suddenly become friendly or involved with a hairdresser, after she has done the imagery, who colours her hair for her. Often with self-imagery, the way or means to creating the end result, occurs in an unexpected manner.

Self-imagery can take many forms. As an example, look at someone who has had plastic surgery. A person who has changed their appearance has done so because they have a different self-image of themselves than what they were born with. Because they want to see themselves differently, they have recreated themselves with plastic surgery.

If you truly put some time, energy and focus into self-imagery and imagery, and put twenty minutes aside each day to do this, you'll be truly amazed at what arises and occurs in your life. I have found that through practising this 'mind art', self-imagery has an ability to set the wheels in motion and get things going on cosmic levels of operation that are quite phenomenal. Let me give you an example. I know I can envisage myself travelling or being in some special place. Or I may talk to people about a place they have visited, and remark on how much I would love to go there. Mentally, within a week or two of me mentioning some place I would love to visit, the phone will ring and some opportunity, job or whatever will arise to take me to that location. Now it is one of those strange situations that occurs when you start to practise mental thinking. Your thoughts turn into reality. If you asked me how this happens, I can't tell you the answers because there are no real explanations about how or why self-imagery or imagery works—these conditions operate on the subconscious realms of existence. However, I know that they do work and I acknowledge that the ways of the unconscious—the hidden depths of ourselves—are truly mysterious. What I am trying to impart and share with you is that there is no need to think small when it comes to self-imagery or imagery. In fact, I try not to limit myself at all! I often 'image' something that would appear to be totally impossible, only to discover that it is very possible, although (as with the girl with the hairpieces mentioned above), it may occur in a different form than I expected.

Therefore, even if you are very short and want to be taller, this can be 'yours' in all manner of ways. For example, certain clothes create the illusion of a 'taller' appearance, and it may be this new way of dressing that your 'taller look' will take shape. But you might not find the means to look taller until you begin the imagery. The imagery seems to attract the right information or opportunities to fulfill your desires to you. Just imagining yourself looking a certain way, being in a certain place, or being with a certain person, works the magic. This mental thinking somehow seems to attract the means to achieve that dimension of yourself in a form of 'reality' where you appear in that situation or position, even if not in true 'actuality'. Therefore, don't feel foolish mentally imagining yourself as slim, toned, tall, short, long-haired, short-haired, smooth-skinned, or whatever it is you would love to see yourself look like. Instead, have fun and enjoy self-imaging and be grateful for seeing yourself looking so wonderful in your own inner imagery. Feel all the senses of that situation occurring for you. For example, as mentioned earlier, the more you imagine yourself as beautiful, successful, popular, or whatever it is that you desire, in your own special way, and with all the benefits that these states of beauty, success or popularity give (both inwardly and outwardly), the more your desire will become a reality. By feeling every 'essence' or spectrum of the experience and claiming it as your own and part of your vibrational frequency, the reality will appear around you to match your feelings. Just watch. After imaging yourself as 'gorgeous', someone will suddenly turn to you and say, 'You are looking gorgeous today' or 'Hello, gorgeous'. It is amazing how these things happen, and they will.

Here is a warning about the attitudes or beliefs that will hold you back and work against your imaging process. This is like using a magic energy in reverse against you.

When you tell yourself, or others, that you hate your bottom, you hate your hair, you wish you were taller and so on, you are actually not helping yourself. In fact, you are using imagery in the reverse process. You are working against your own self-development and betterment. It is very important not to put yourself down. Being down on yourself doesn't honour the incredible spark of cosmic creativity that you represent in the universe at all. The sooner you begin to believe that you are beautiful, the quicker you will become that way!

This may come as a stretch for some readers, but you are better off being grateful for being overweight, rather than upset about it.

Being overweight is likely to have taught you some wonderful lessons in your life. Or, for all you know, your 'overweight' issue may be serving a higher purpose in your life. Who knows? If you believe in the higher powers, you know that you have been created exactly as you are meant to be for now, at least. If you are overweight, it could be a gift to you—it may have been designed to teach you humility or to give you the motivation and desire to learn to love and value your individual worth more. Being overweight may truly be your greatest teacher because, in life, some of our greatest gifts or blessings often come in strange disguises. But that doesn't mean you have to stay overweight. Once you have learnt your lessons, you can move on from this state of being. But note that loving yourself, respecting yourself and honouring yourself are very important components of creating true change in your life. When you love yourself exactly as you are, you have real power—the power to change yourself. As long as you are angry and upset with yourself, you are holding yourself back.

Chapter Ten
Practise Being Grateful

I firmly believe that whatever we are grateful for in life serves us and whatever we are resentful towards (including the parts of our own body), end up working and going against us.

Athena

I have seen this phenomenon of gratitude versus resentment affect many individuals at various times in their life. I have observed people who have made themselves, and even others around them, extremely ill by harbouring resentment and bitterness toward themselves or others. Alternatively, I have seen individuals who have been grateful, who have healed themselves and all those around them, in the process of being grateful.

Grateful people definitely seem to be more beautiful than those who are bitter. The individual who is grateful and thankful radiates a spiritual glow while those who are bitter, resentful and ungrateful seem to shrivel up. No matter what is going on in life, whatever it may be, the wise person remains grateful for everything. Gratitude and a positive frame of mind help things get better and can, indeed, change any negative situation if you allow time to do its work.

Adopting an attitude of gratitude will create miracles and magic in your life.

Being grateful creates all kinds of positive energy around you. It expands your psychic powers and helps you focus your mind on creating a better 'you'. When you are unhappy, dissatisfied or dispirited you attract problems. When you are grateful, you attract opportunities. You look much better when you are filled with gratitude than when you are down in the dumps. Having loads of negative brain noise ticking in your head is distracting and often painful. It can lead to a negative state of mind that can be quite destructive. As a result you end up being upset or feeling unhappy with the way you look, your body shape, or having the perception that you lack sex appeal. This is self-defeating. No matter what you think about yourself, remember that confidence is the rocket fuel of life—and you won't have confidence at all if you constantly perceive yourself and your life in the negative.

Chapter Eleven
Your Body Speaks Out!

We put on weight in the areas of our body that are the physical energy centres for our troubled emotional and psychological expression. Athena

Many people ask why certain parts of their body are the first place to put on weight, while other body areas remain slim? I believe this is because every area of the body is subconsciously linked to a specific emotion. Psychic healers (and even some extremely intuitive medical doctors) treat their patients with the knowledge that our bodies are directly linked to our mind's condition.

Our thoughts, problems or worries directly affect and influence certain body areas. It seems impractical and unwise to expect to treat the effect of poor condition in anybody's physical body, such as an illness or a tendency to be overweight, without looking for its psychological cause.

The question should be asked: 'What is making this person ill?' or 'What is making this person put on weight?' Cause and effect should be considered! When looking at weight gain, I believe we put on weight in the areas of our body that are the physical energy centres for our troubled emotional and psychological expression. When we feel psychologically or emotionally vulnerable or sense we need to protect ourselves in some fashion, the part of our body which aligns, attunes and is 'emotionally coded' with this vulnerable feeling, is where we attract the weight gain.

We are putting up our defenses in a physical fashion.

In short, weight gain is the way we put on our psychological and bodily armour to protect ourselves from the world.

Matching Emotion to Areas of Your Body

Naturally each person is unique and different, and there can be many varied reasons for weight gain, which are not simply psychological or emotional. However, the emotions and body area links I list below are those derived from extensive discussions, consultations and astrological readings I have had with people in order to find what emotional beliefs match to specific areas of the body. It is easy to see where you tend to gain weight if you experience any of the emotions below and what you can do to change this.

The Stomach = Survival

The stomach area houses our gut instincts. It is where we receive our messages to either flee or fight when faced with a confrontation. It represents the survival area of the body. A lot of psychic fears can build up in our tummies. Consequently, when an individual feels afraid of the future because they fear the unknown, or are afraid of being hurt (either physically or emotionally), they put on weight around the tummy area.

Sometimes even very thin people have quite protruding tummies. People who have a protruding or fat tummy are often harbouring deep-seated fears of being 'abandoned'. This individual sometimes feels unloved, or unlovable with the possibility that one of their parents was not affectionate, reassuring or accessible to them emotionally. They are often overly generous, giving and kind to others in a subconscious attempt to get others to return love to them.

The Backside = Trust in Life

Our backside has a lot to do with trust. Being positioned on the rear side of the body, it is connected with what is past, as the front area of the body has a lot to do with what is the future.

When a person feels they have no support or that they have been constantly let down by others in the past, or even stabbed in the back, their body often compensates for this by putting on weight on the backside. If you feel you have nothing or nobody to depend on, or fall back on in life, or others haven't been there in the past for you when you needed them, then this part of your anatomy often overcompensates for this sense of lack of trust by becoming more protrusive.

The derriere is our psychological back up—something to fall back on. When you have a lot of weight on your derriere, in many ways you are covering your own butt or back.

The Legs = The Future and Our Progress

Our legs are what carry us forward through life. They connect us to our feet and the earth. Our legs link us to ground-bound reality. When someone has very weighty legs all over, it indicates they are afraid of what the future holds and/or feels that they need to provide for themselves a strong physical or bodily link to reality and the earth.

People with heavy legs may be unconsciously afraid of their own thought patterns, or of being swept away from everyday practicality or reality by their heart's deeper passions or their mind's more audacious fantasies. These individuals are attempting to balance their upper torso energies with their lower torso energies, by providing a ballast or an anchor through their legs. They are firmly imploding themselves on solid ground. In psychological terms, they are attaching themselves rigidly to the earth.

The Upper Legs or Thighs = Personal Power

When an individual has very weighty upper legs or thighs (sometimes noticeably out of proportion to their lower legs), this indicates a belief or fear that they don't have enough personal power or stamina to organise, discipline or carry out life's everyday demands. They feel that, 'I have to take care of myself', or 'I must do whatever it takes and/or necessary to survive'. Heavy upper legs or thighs means this person is attempting to summon all the power they can to defend themselves on all levels of existence.

The Lower Leg = Self-worth Issues

When an individual has very weighty lower legs (sometimes noticeably out of proportion to their upper legs or thighs), this indicates a deep-seated sense of unworthiness. This person often has a sibling in their family who is a big rival for them— possibly someone who is very successful in life, attractive or has outshone them in some fashion during their early years (and probably someone who has a very slim torso). This individual is often harbouring a sense of 'not being good enough' or of always playing second fiddle or being second best. They can suffer from the anxiety that they are not attractive enough to be loved for who they are.

The Ankles = Freedom of Movement

Our ankles give us the ability to be flexible and to twist and turn as we move. When individuals have very thick, fat ankles, they are concerned that they may get lost in some way or be left alone to cope on their own.

This person often has a very deep-seated fear about change and doesn't want to go through any sort of transition period in their lives. As a consequence, they are often found in jobs they don't like doing or in relationships with people that are totally unsuited to them.

People with thick or fat ankles frequently feel 'different' from everybody else—as though they are in a realm or a league of their own, sometimes even playing the role of the black sheep in their family dynamics. It is also very likely they believe that others don't really understand or value them for who they truly are.

Quite often these people have a parent who died when they were young or have been lost as an infant or always in the company of a babysitter or even fostered and have never forgotten the experience.

The Arms = Our Desires

The arms are the part of the body that really connect us (and provide physical access) to the world around us. We reach out and embrace others and our environment with our arms. When we feel we can't reach out far enough or hold enough of others or the world around us, we tend to put on weight on our arms to compensate for this sense of emptiness. Heavy arms also indicate an inability to connect closely with others as the arms have a lot to do with intimacy. We can get closer to others or wrap around others with our arms. When a person is afraid that they will be rejected and pushed away from life in some fashion, they often put on weight in their arms to compensate.

The Fingers and Hands = Worried About Possessions

When we put weight on our fingers or hands, it is because we are afraid of an opportunity slipping through our fingers, and we are attempting to compensate for the fact that we feel we have lost our ability to hold onto things such as money, relationships, assets, independence or other forms of material or spiritual possessions. Individuals with fat fingers are often extremely fearful about loss in whatever form 'loss' takes or represents for them.

The Neck = Communication

When people feel that they aren't being heard or that others either ignore their point of view or don't listen to them, they often put on weight under the neckline. They have deep-seated issues about communication operating within them.

This person may be nursing beliefs that they are stupid, unintelligent or poorly educated and may have been told this repeatedly as a child by a parent, schoolteacher, or other children. This 'you are stupid' response may have even been continued by their adult partner later on in life.

Weight gain in this area of the body can be a way of saying 'I don't care if you don't listen to what I am saying', when in fact, they truly do care what other people think and how much attention others are paying or not paying to them. Often this individual is likely to feel that what they have to say has little value or worth to anyone else.

The Face = The Focus

This is the individual who feels a lack of self-importance and inwardly has an inferiority complex (even if they are very successful in worldly terms).

Subliminally, they are attempting to make themselves bigger and better to others. When people have lots of weight on their faces, it means they feel they need to give or offer more of themselves to the world around them.

Like in nature, when a lizard puffs up its face to frighten or attract other friends or foes, a big face also attracts attention. This person is subconsciously saying, 'Notice me!' On unconscious levels, this person is attempting to be important.

Entire Body Overweight = Separated from Love

When someone's entire body is overweight, psychologically they want to put up every barrier between themselves and the world around them. They are extremely afraid of being hurt and unloved, and in fact probably consciously believe that nobody loves them when the reality is that they don't truly love themselves. This weight is their armour against the world and it isn't until they learn to have more trust, faith and love in themselves that they will let this weight go and walk slim, proud and tall.

Chapter Twelve
Your Zodiac Eating Habits

Using the principles of astrology can provide some amazing insights as to why certain people do the things they do when it comes to eating.

Aries—The Munchers

Aries can range from an Olive Oyl shape to a jolly Humphrey B. Bear size. It's easy for an Aries to be either taut and muscular, or overly pudgy, but not necessarily fit with just being naturally toned. Aries can be all-or-nothing kind of people when it comes to food and fitness. Ruled by Mars, it is almost a 'must-do' pre-requisite for this sign to burn up energy and keep busy, otherwise they burn out mentally, emotionally and physically. Exercise can help Aries maintain their most productive and attractive weight levels. If you see a thin Aries who doesn't exercise, they may be suffering from major mental angst, a form of ill health, or have been through some kind of drama that has affected their metabolism or internal health status. A healthy, energetic Aries is often plumper than they enjoy being. Sensual in nature, Aries often look forward to their next meal with high anticipation, but generally, they do not enjoy preparing food themselves. Munchers who love to crunch away on foods with texture, Aries enjoy having a full stomach. It is surprising that we do not see more heavy-set people born under this sign, but being such a mentally and physically active sign, they generally run or burn their weight off with activity. However, when an Aries slows down, and especially if they are avid television viewers, they soon become couch potatoes. Whether young or old, as Aries become irritable when they are hungry, it is best to feed them quickly, rather than keep them waiting.

Taurus—The Self-indulgers

Ruled by Venus, the most pleasure-oriented planet, Taurus is innately born with a sweet tooth, which is why this sign often battles with the bulge. Willpower can be tough for pleasure-loving Taurus to summon up, and when a Taurean tries to diet they usually bore quickly of their need to constantly say 'no' to second helpings or any kind of temptation. In fact, many a Taurean's life revolves around where their next joyous (and highly anticipated) meal is coming from—and their fantasies can revolve around what their next morsel will be. Many Taureans are very big eaters. That's why you will see many Taureans at spas and health gyms working overtime to lose a few kilograms, only to go out after their workout and indulge in a double chocolate sundae. Lovers of all foods, but particularly when it comes to desserts, statistically more Taureans are employed as professional chefs and authors of cookbooks than any other sign of the zodiac.

Gemini—All or Nothing Eaters

The tick tock, operating like the swing of the pendulum, Geminis live up to their dualistic twin nature by either eating everything in sight or picking at whatever is on their plates. They are very much either into food or turned off by it—depending on their palates. Sometimes if they are busy, Geminis skip meals altogether and wonder why they run out of energy before the day is through. Most of the things that are naturally bad for them—chocolate, coffee, alcohol and cigarettes—are often the things they enjoy the most and crave. However, many Geminis do find that abstinence in these areas is their own true pathway towards health, so they can be very strict vegetarians and self-aware health-watchers too. There is a need for Geminis to be careful with their intake because they often have physical weaknesses that become more pronounced if they neglect their well-being. Many Geminis need to carefully think about and plan their diets and watch their eating habits, because these areas of their lives can quickly spin out of control causing them ongoing problems before they know it. Operating on nervous energy, Geminis often eat on the run, or have strange food desires, unusual snacks, or many beverages (like abundant cups of strong coffee) throughout the day. Overeating (and sometimes drinking and smoking) can become the Gemini's outlet for nervous energy. On a final note, from my own observations, Geminis tend to rate high on the statistical list of anorexics.

Cancer—The Moody Eaters

Emotionally oriented Cancers live their life in ongoing phases of highs and lows, likes and dislikes, weight gains and weight losses. They go through many stages and phases in their lives, similar to the moon, which rules them. This means Cancers can experience cycles of erratic eating patterns where they either love or hate food. Their moods can dictate whether they turn every day into a food fest, where they can't wait to put some tasty morsel into their mouths, or if they will ignore food altogether. They can even go into extremes where they'll feel sick when they are around food or cannot stand the smell of certain dishes. Because of their vacillating moods and desires, often you'll find their refrigerator stacked either full of goodies or amazingly empty, and this occurs because the Cancer's moods have the ability to swing so dramatically back and forth. However, symbolically, food represents security to Cancers because it has a lot to do with family, nurturing, feeling loved and being comfortable. As Cancer is the sign of the zodiac that rules the stomach, everything that goes into their tummy has a profound impact on them. Eating excessively can be their outlet for emotional turmoil, especially if they have been through tough times, such as a marriage breakup, a job disappointment or have financial worries. I have noticed over the years that many Cancers tend to suffer from bulimia (think of Princess Diana).

Leo—Feast or Famine Eaters

The way to a Leo's heart is often through their stomach! No wonder so many Leos end up at the weight loss clinic, disappointed with the fact that they are looking pudgy and overweight. Their usual way of dieting is to go on strict fasts or to abstain from food and alcohol altogether (they tend to be an all-or-nothing kind of sign). However, if they do go on diets, they can lose interest with any diet very quickly and return to eating in abundance again before too long has passed because they get bored. It isn't easy for Leos to be disciplined, although their vanity often helps them accomplish this trait. Being extravagant in nature and also self-indulgent, Leos generally do not like to deny themselves any pleasures, particularly food. Indeed, most Leos are hearty eaters, but many also like to have the finest foods rather than just a lot of food. Leos like the finest of everything and the same applies to whatever it is they put on their plates. Fine food and wine is often what expands their waists very quickly, especially if they decline from exercising regularly. Food often plays an enormous role in their lives. They also like to make their meals a special occasion and are often extremely social and enjoy great success in playing the host. What makes a meal exceptional or memorable for them is the presentation of the food, the company they are in, the wine that accompanies the meal, and where it is served. If Leos cook themselves, they usually have a great sense of style and presentation about it. Dinner parties at their homes can turn into a performance, a show, a drama, or something that is talked about for a long time afterwards.

Virgo—Fussy Eaters

Get out the tape measure, weigh everything you intend to eat on the scales, and generally keep a close watch over those calories. Most Virgos are statisticians and watchers of the small stuff in life by nature—and when it comes to food, diets and health fads or trends, Virgos generally know a great deal about everything and anything about them—or maybe even have attended classes or written papers on them. Virgos are 'into' health. They are often caretakers of others, work in the health industry or assist in helping others to get healthy. This career direction often stems from their own concerns over their general wellbeing. Many Virgos are hypochondriacs who have their bathroom shelves stacked with every kind of health vitamin or painkiller. If you go to any health food shop you're likely to find plenty of Virgos shopping there or actually running or owning the establishment. Quite often Virgos are fussy eaters. They prefer to avoid exotic or unknown foods where possible, and like to stick to the healthy foods or spices they know or their parents used before them. The more basic, healthy and simple their food and diet is, the better they feel towards it. Often they feel guilty (or even suffer from nausea) if they eat fatty foods or desserts. Simplicity can be their idea of dining perfection. More vegetarians and health food fanatics are born under this sign than any other. Virgos can also suffer from acute constipation, nervous problems and stomach upsets quite regularly.

Libra—Pleasure Seeking Eaters

Ruled by Venus, Librans are supposed to be the most ardent pleasure seekers of the zodiac. They also tend to be indulgent and super-lazy when it comes to exercise. No wonder so many Librans end up moaning and groaning about how much weight they have gained recently, especially around the festive season, with no one to blame but themselves for their overindulgence. 'If it is good to taste, then it should be good for you' is often the Libran's food intake motto, but of course, this attitude doesn't apply or work in real life at all. When you open the door of many a Libran's refrigerator and see what is waiting to be enjoyed, it can be like a smorgasbord of sensual delight. The abundance of pleasure loitering in their refrigerator can be quite a foodfest for the eyes to behold and the stomach to savour. Sadly, for Librans, the best tasting things frequently turn out to be those food items that add on weight very quickly, so the Libran has to carefully watch what they eat, rather than just simply taste and say, 'this is terrific, so give me some more of it!' Cooking can be a profession or hobby for this sign. As Libra is the sign of the trend-maker or setter, they are often into food styles or preparation that are different or up to the minute in some fashion. Being good cooks, they like to show their originality and style by serving dishes from France or something with sophistication and flair attached to it. They can be veritable health food gourmets too, often baking their own breads or making their own pasta. The same applies to what they drink—it will either be juices or herbal teas (if their inkling is toward health foods) or the best wines or French champagne.

Scorpio—Power Eaters

You will meet Scorpios who are hugely overweight and others who closely watch every morsel that crosses their lips. This sign is very much fixed on being super-indulgent or super-disciplined, and usually there is no real in between ground for them. Scorpios definitely have a will of their own and it is hard for others to advise or influence them. As Scorpio is the sign which rules passion, intensity and overwhelming desire, should a Scorpio really get into food (or a certain type of food), they really get into it and overeat. Fortunately, that same passionate attitude can be applied to maintaining a healthy lifestyle or diet. If they decide to devote themselves to living a healthy existence or keeping to a fixed diet, they do it well. This sign can have an intense nature all of its own—which no other sign can beat. They can also become obsessive about their food preferences. If you are inviting a Scorpio over for dinner, it is wise to inquire in advance about their food preferences. Scorpio is the black and white sign of the zodiac, with no grey area at all. They have fixed opinions and once they are set on a course, it can take a great deal of outside pressure to shift them over to a different way of looking at life. So if a Scorpio has a weight problem, it can be tough for them to break their patterns of eating, but once they succeed in doing this shift, they can then be very firmly fixed on a new direction and achieve amazing results.

Sagittarius—Back for Seconds Eaters

The 'more the merrier' is the general rule for good living for Sagittarians. This same philosophy often describes what happens when they load up their plates with food. Unless they are athletic in nature, which many Sagittarians are fortunate enough to be, you will find many people under this sign overweight. Being active and keeping an ongoing flow of exercise in their lives is very important to this sign, otherwise they tend to become very slow movers. Unfortunately, for this gregarious sign, a Sagittarian's body just seems to be set naturally to a slow metabolic rate that makes them add on extra kilos very quickly, unless they maintain a regular exercise regime or closely monitor their food intake. Ruled by Jupiter, the planet of enjoyment and excess, when a Sagittarian gets hungry, they are super hungry. Socially oriented, most Sagittarians are born loving food and the total dining experience. They love the whole thing of sitting around a table with a drink in one hand and a fork in the other, telling jokes and tales about their conquests or the things that have occurred throughout the day. Dieting for a Sagittarian can be hard and some find dieting quite impossible to maintain. Removing them from their food fun can be like taking a duck away from water. That's why a shift in their mental attitude or perspective is the only way they can often sustain a balanced diet and comfortable body weight. More than any other sign of the zodiac, Sagittarian's need to 'think themselves thin!'

Capricorn—Sensible Eaters

Although many Capricorns indulge in junk food and sometimes learn their lessons for health, wellbeing and weight gain the hard way, the majority of Capricorns usually realise early in life that it is wise for them to eat well. They usually have learnt from illnesses or health upsets in the past, how important it is to take care of their fitness and wellbeing. Capricorns are strong individuals, physically, but the wrong diet can quickly sap away their energy flow and even run them down. This sign is attuned to physical realms (and their physical self), and they can see or feel very quickly what foods slow them down and what foods give them vigour. Discipline is usually something they are born with too, with Capricorns generally being serious and not flippant. This sense of self-survival or self-protectiveness helps them become more aware of when they are overdoing anything or acting irresponsibly. Not that their diligence with eating or drinking is always close to perfection—there are many Capricorns who wage a battle with the bulge all their lives and lose it. But if they are fortunate enough to live in a stable environment and are in a job they enjoy, and have a partner they feel secure with, a Capricorn can be very serious about maintaining a good, healthy lifestyle. However, if any area of their life is unfulfilled or they are faced with stress, they can slip into extremely poor eating and exercise habits. Lovers of fresh foods, many a Capricorn's garden is filled with fresh herbs, tomatoes and vegetables, all organically grown to provide them with inner fortitude to face the world. Capricorns are great hosts and generally are fabulous cooks. They operate and feel best when they avoid overindulging in salt, sugar, alcohol and ice-cream.

Aquarius—Creatures of Habit Eaters

Many Aquarians like to live their life by the clock and have a fixed food or exercise schedule that they stick to, unless something extraordinary occurs in their life which cartwheels their well-laid plans to uncharted or unexpected directions. The same applies to their eating habits or trends. As they do not like change, it is not unusual for Aquarians to eat the exact same breakfast, lunch or dinner everyday. They often sit down at exactly the same time of day (almost to the second) to eat their selected food or tidbits. Creatures of habit, Aquarians do not generally enjoy surprises, particularly when it comes to food. They love things to be pre-dictable and enjoy having the same meal cooked the same way at the same time—and if things are not done that way, it can be quite stressful for them. My father, who was an Aquarian, used to want his potatoes cooked exactly the same way each day—boiled for a certain amount of minutes—and my mother (a Virgo) used to fuss about making sure they were cooked exactly on time for him to sit down and listen to the news while he ate his dinner! If she varied the procedure in any form or fashion, he would know! He was psychic when it came to the preparation of his food. Usually Aquarians are not into cooking for pleasure themselves, but they will cook to have something to eat. They can be content eating little snacks or having cheese on crackers with a cup of tea or a glass of wine. This type of nibble food is enough to tide them over until a real meal comes their way—either an evening out or a meal prepared by someone else.

Pisces—Sweet Eaters

You'll find many overweight Pisceans on our planet. They tend to live for their eating delights and all the things they shouldn't eat are often high on their food agenda of most desirable goodies. Pisceans have limited discipline, so unless they are born with a slim, trim body as a result of their genes, they can be often found facing a dilemma when it comes to trying to lose weight. They get a tremendous amount of psychological pleasure from indulging in food. Food can be a kind of therapy for Pisceans, so they need to find food that is healthy and good for them, which often they cannot seem to do. When they are fatigued or drained, Pisceans will indulge in all the wrong food temptations, so this is the time when they should choose their energy foods very wisely. Sweet dreams hold a special meaning for some Pisceans, and can lead to them going to bed at night, loaded up with chocolate, biscuits and other delicacies. Many Pisceans have a love–hate affair with food. They love to eat up big, but hate the fact that when they do, they put on weight. Many Pisceans use eating to ease their troubled minds, which is why so many of them are constantly going on a diet. However, when a Piscean puts on a lot of weight and keeps it on, it can be an indication that they are protecting themselves and using their weight as armour against the outside world.

Chapter Thirteen
Your Astro-Guide to Making Fitness More Fun!

Knowing your zodiac sign's personality traits can help you lose weight! Athena

When you use your mind powers to 'think thin', there is no need to exercise or go on a diet. But, if you want to achieve quick and long-lasting results, everything helps. So if you want to speed up your slimming regime, Chapter Thirteen may prove useful in making your wish for a bod-delicious figure come true!

It's good to be strong-minded! This one factor can help you create miracles in your life and in the lives of others. It can be exhilarating to use your own mind powers and innermost will to help yourself lose weight and achieve other goals. But feeling terrific, and looking toned and radiant, is hugely dependent on upgrading the state of your physical health and fitness. It can take some effort to do this over the long term—and that's why it can be helpful to look at ways to exercise in a manner that suits your own values and needs. Knowing about your star sign can help you improve your general wellbeing and achieve fitness goals by doing activities that flow easily and happily for you. Using the principles of astrology, here are some astro-insights on upgrading your fitness levels and, best of all, having fun while you do it.

Aries

Remember your schoolteachers who scolded you to curb your natural enthusiasm and said, 'Walk! Don't run!' Well, it's time to forget those deeply embedded orders and go back to your natural way of doing things. A true Aries doesn't saunter casually and nonchalantly through the day. You're a fire sign, and an energy person, so you are happiest when you can run, skip and jump around, burning all your fiery energy! Set free the fun-loving side of your personality—lace up your running shoes and zip through your list of errands so you have time to check out a few of your favourite shops before you head home. Turn your household chores into Olympic events. Set a new record in the 'sweeper sprint' and bring home the gold in the 'grocery shopping dash'.

Your Fitness Strengths and Weaknesses

Most Aries are born with natural speed and endurance. Your astro-symbol, the Ram, is known for its amazing resilience, but you should learn to pace yourself, rather than going full speed ahead and burning out quickly. Your sign can also be vulnerable to head injuries and sprains, so take care to protect yourself by wearing the proper helmets and equipment for both work and play.

Fitness Tips

Stay away from your refrigerator when you're bored, and don't shop for groceries when you are hungry. Boredom is the worst enemy of an Aries, so make sure you have a plan for your day or you could end up flipping through the television channels while you mindlessly polish off all the chips and chocolate in the pantry.

If you're struggling with excess weight, or you have so much energy that you can't sit still, add some excitement to your life with a new sport or hobby. You like to be helpful too, so consider turning good deeds into fitness by taking your dog (or someone else's) for a walk, help an elderly neighbour by doing their shopping for them, or volunteer to assist on a school excursion.

How to Reward Yourself

You thrive on competition and rewards, so set fitness goals that challenge you to do your best. To stay motivated, sign up for some fun or recreational competitions that give every participant a ribbon or certificate. Your astro-sign loves prizes, new toys, trendy fashions, and the latest crazes, so reward yourself with whatever you want most and enjoy!

Taurus

The next time you have the urge to 'shop till you drop' slip into your most comfortable walking shoes, don your best-looking casuals, and head for your favourite malls, collectible shops and flea markets. Most Taureans collect something or other, so have fun getting fit while you search for treasures to complete your collections. Get the most mileage out of your day by parking a block or two away from your final destination and make frequent trips back and forth to your car to stash your new purchases. When it comes to housework, turn on some music and dance your way through your chores. When the slow songs come on, take a break, relax your neck and shoulders and stretch your legs and back.

Your Fitness Strengths and Weaknesses

Like your astro-symbol, the Bull, you are strong and persistent and these two characteristics can work to your greatest advantage when you direct them toward your fitness. Your sign is sometimes prone to leg injuries, so focus on strengthening your legs through hiking, swimming or some other gentle, strength-building activities. Ruled by Venus, Taurus loves pleasure, so your greatest weakness is often your temptation to overindulge.

Fitness Tips

Slow and steady may not always win the race, but it sure beats fast and miserable—especially for Taureans. Intensive work-outs are great for some zodiac signs, but they definitely aren't suited to the typical Taurean. Trade-in rigorous routines for sports and activities that are slow-paced and less physically demanding. Eat several small meals a day, instead of trying to starve yourself. If you begin to feel deprived, take care of the craving right away by enjoying a moderate portion of one of your favourite foods—guilt free!

How to Reward Yourself

Your sign carries around a great deal of responsibility and many of your decisions are based on what you 'should' do, rather than on what you 'love' to do. The rewards you give yourself for achieving your fitness goals work best when they are completely and totally selfish. This is the perfect opportunity to put yourself first. Stay on your fitness track by setting up a plan loaded with incentives!

Gemini

The twins of the zodiac can easily do two things at the same time, so combining fitness with fun is right up your alley. Take advantage of your special talent by reading the morning paper while you spin the pedals of your exercise bike, tune in to your favourite sitcom while you walk on the spot, or do gentle stretches as you fold and iron the laundry. Whether you're at work or at home, develop the muscles in your upper body by sitting and standing with a straight posture and walking tall, even when you're alone. Instead of chatting to your friends on the telephone, meet them for a walk in the park or an outing at the beach or zoo.

Your Fitness Strengths and Weaknesses

You have enough energy for two people and you're often a step ahead of your peers, both in your actions and in your way of thinking. It's important to efficiently use up your energy in productive activities or your strength can become your greatest weakness. Pent up energy turns to anxiety in your delicate nervous system and this can lead to late-night bingeing, or other unhealthy habits such as smoking.

Fitness Tips

One of the best ways for you to boost your fitness level is to team up with a friend, or group of friends, to play a sport, dance, or attend an aerobics class together. A social atmosphere makes it easy for you to get into shape and you'll barely notice the effort compared to exercising on your own. With Mercury as your ruling planet, you do a lot of rushing around. So make sure you always have healthy, low fat food in the house so you can eat and run—otherwise, the temptation to grab fast food on the road will seriously slow down your fitness fun and progress.

How to Reward Yourself

You love the thrill of achieving your goals and while you don't need recognition, you do love it! Make sure you let your family and friends in on your fitness goals and celebrate your ongoing success with them by getting together for a movie or some other form of entertainment that isn't centred around food. Reward your accomplishments by dressing up and dancing the night away at your favourite nightclub, or indulge in a healthy salad at the most chic restaurant in the city.

Cancer

The best way for you to have fun getting into shape is to keep your options open so you can seize opportunities to combine work with fitness when they present themselves. The first step is to put aside your stack of exercise books and listen to your body. It is not wise for you to plan too far ahead, because on some days you'll be raring to go, while on other days, your body may need to rest and recuperate. Build flexibility into your schedule so you can take a break from your work to walk to a nearby café for a healthy snack or pack a light lunch and spend your lunch hour window shopping or running errands. Whenever possible, take the stairs instead of the elevator, and when you're waiting in a queue, or someone puts you on hold, practice deep and relaxed breathing to release tension from your mind and body.

Your Fitness Strengths and Weaknesses

It's no surprise that nearly all Cancerians have great legs! With gentle and consistent conditioning and stretching, your legs can carry you anywhere you want to go. Be careful not to let this asset turn into your Achilles heel by ignoring fatigue and pushing yourself beyond your natural limits. Take good care of your hands and feet to avoid calluses, blisters and any other annoying conditions that can sabotage your fitness plans, and save your mile-high heels for very special occasions.

Fitness Tips

Don't let fitness trainers or exercise fanatics talk you into establishing a set routine. You respond most favourably to spontaneous exercise that allows you to determine the amount of effort your body should exert. You know your own limits, so stay within yourself, whether you're working or playing. When it comes to losing weight, the advice for a Cancerian is simple—eat when you are hungry and don't eat when you're not! Ignore traditional meal times and when you're at home, make it a habit to use medium or small plates for meals, rather than large dinner plates.

How to Reward Yourself

It is very important to set your goals in small steps and reward yourself frequently for your progress. Rather than gauging your progress by the actual amount of kilograms lost, check your fitness level by how you feel and how your clothing fits. When you go down a size, reward yourself with a sexy dress or fashion fad that flatters your figure. Also pay attention to your increase in strength and stamina and reward yourself when tasks, such as carrying shopping bags or lifting laundry baskets, become noticeably easier. Pampering yourself for your accomplishments is one of the best ways to ensure your fitness fun and success!

Leo

For a Leo, getting into shape is a lot more fun when you do it with a bunch of other people! You tend to operate on a grand scale, so if you are planning to raise your fitness level, use your natural leadership talents and organise a group of friends and co-workers to join you! When you're working around the house, play harmonious music, pretend you have an audience and perform your chores with dramatic flair and grace to gently develop your muscles and improve your strength and poise. Leos love to go to new places and see new things, so rack up some fitness mileage by touring your various museums and galleries, checking out new shopping centres, or exploring local parks and recreational areas.

Your Fitness Strengths and Weaknesses

Your astro-symbol, the Lion, is a reflection of your great physical strength and endurance. Like a lion, you really know how to kick back and make yourself comfortable and relax when time allows. It's very important for you to take time to unwind because stress and fatigue can affect a Leo's back muscles, spine and heart. When you exercise, be sure to set a moderate rhythm for yourself and choose aerobic exercises that involve flowing, rather than jarring movements.

Fitness Tips

Your fitness level can skyrocket when you join a sports team and develop a sense of loyalty to the other players. Your level of effort and ability tends to go up when others are relying on you, and you love rising to the challenge to hit the winning run or score the final goal as the buzzer sounds. To help your body dissolve excess weight, graze on ripened fruits and vegetables and eat more rice and other grains.

How to Reward Yourself

As a proud Leo, you love pomp and circumstance and being the centre of attention, so competing in fitness events can really jump-start your incentive to take advantage of your daily fitness opportunities. You feel depressed when you deny yourself any of your favourite foods, so end your evening meal with a cup of low fat pudding, a glass of wine, or a small bowl of low fat frozen yoghurt. Getting fit is much more fun when you feel triumphant and satisfied at the end of each day.

Virgo

Health and fitness can feel like serious matters to a Virgo, but the best way for you to have fun is to lighten up and let yourself go! When you're doing the chores, pop a funny movie on and laugh your way to fitness while you tidy up the house. When you're at work, close your office door a few times a day and do some sit-ups, push-ups or toe-touches to burn some nervous energy and to keep stress from building up. Once every two weeks, take a personal day from your responsibilities and spend the entire day outdoors with your friends, your family or all by yourself.

Your Fitness Strengths and Weaknesses

Virgo is an extraordinarily healthy sign and you can maintain fitness routines that are more demanding than for some of the other signs. However, your nervous system is sometimes highly strung, so you should take care to practise relaxation techniques. To keep your system in balance, stretch and relax your muscles as much as you exert them. Wear loose-fitting clothing while you exercise, and play sports that avoid you chaffing your skin.

Fitness Tips

The best way for you to get fit is to lighten up your serious nature and let yourself have fun. Laughter is one of the best fitness medicines because it releases stress, lifts your mood, tones your tummy muscles and burns calories. Avoid eating when you're upset or nervous because Virgos are prone to ailments such as stomach ulcers. Your healthiest choice, when you're feeling emotional, is to exercise lightly, so take a long slow walk or snatch a cat nap.

How to Reward Yourself

You are your own biggest critic so it is extremely important for you to reap the rewards of your accomplishments, otherwise you just won't have much fun! Set definite goals pertaining to your strength, flexibility, muscle tone and overall feeling of health and fitness. When possible, buy your upcoming reward ahead of time and place it in plain view—but don't open it until you have reached your goal! Seeing your reward right in front of you will motivate you to jump on every fitness opportunity.

Libra

Leave your old fitness phobias behind and start having some good healthy fun. Fitness no longer means eating what you don't want, drinking what you don't like and doing what you'd prefer not to do! For a Libran, turning on some great music can magically transform ordinary household chores into fitness fun. On sunny days, build your strength by working in the yard planting colourful flowers. You enjoy looking at objects of beauty, including creative architecture and landscapes, so the next time you drive a family member or a friend to a club meeting or sports practice, instead of sitting on the sidelines or running an errand, slip on your gym shoes and take a brisk walk around the neighbourhood.

Your Fitness Strengths and Weaknesses

Your astro-symbol, the Scales, is a reminder that your greatest strength comes from moderation and balance in all areas of your life, including fitness. As an Air sign, your circulatory system is key to your physical wellbeing and it's important to strengthen this system with aerobic activities and plenty of fresh air. Boosting your aerobic ability will also keep you energised. Choose activities that don't put extra stress on your lower back or shoulders because these can be vulnerable areas for you.

Fitness Tips

Ruled by Venus, the planet of beauty and pleasure, Librans respond most favourably to fitness when it's harmoniously combined with music. Start out with dance aerobics and explore all forms of dance that appeal to you. You do best with a bit of routine, so sign up for a class that meets two or three times a week, and make sure the class is on your lunch hour, on your way home from work, or just around the corner from your home. The more convenient fitness is for you, the more likely you will stick to it and enjoy it too!

How to Reward Yourself

It is important for you to clearly see your progress, so reward yourself with clothing and accessories that show you're improving. The better you feel when you look in the mirror, the easier it will be to whistle your way through work and make it on time for dance class! Create a fashion statement by rewarding yourself with all the pieces you need (one article of clothing or an accessory a week) to show your new level of fitness.

Scorpio

Remember those cleaning and home improvement projects that you have wanted to get around to for months? Score some fitness goals by burning up calories re-organising the garage, clearing out the attic, or sprucing up your kitchen with a fresh coat of paint. Consciously think about your posture and the muscles you are using to accomplish your tasks. Pace yourself and don't be overzealous!

At work, jump on any opportunity to deliver messages or run office errands. If you cannot get out of the office, take a two-minute break every hour or so to walk around and stretch your legs.

Fitness Strengths and Weaknesses

The powerful influence of planet Pluto gives Scorpios a strong constitution and resilient immune system. To your great advantage, you are generally stronger than you look, with many Scorpios being agile and light on their feet. Your greatest weakness, in terms of fun fitness, is the 'do or die' approach that works well in some areas of your life, but not so well in the fitness arena. Practising moderation is essential for you to avoid a series of injuries or illness.

Fitness Tips

As a water sign, Scorpio is susceptible to environmental pollutants, so seek out clean air and pure water every chance you get, especially when you're exercising! Take full advantage of your fearless side and learn a thrilling and challenging sport that you've always wanted to try. Avoid getting down in the dumps, because when you're depressed, your famous steely inner willpower can quickly melt under the influence of a cream-filled doughnut or other favourite treat.

How to Reward Yourself

Your Scorpio nature makes you very goal-oriented, so you usually have built-in determination to reach your desired fitness level. That means you can reward yourself with something grand and glorious when you reach your final goals, because you won't need the constant reinforcement of smaller rewards along the way. Raising your fitness level is very valuable for all aspects of your life, so don't short-change yourself on your reward. Make it as great as your success!

Sagittarius

When you came into this world, your first thought was probably a question. You are the zodiac's explorer and your curious nature can put the fun into fitness for you! Spend an afternoon gazing at the exhibits in a museum, flower show or special attraction, or check out all the stores in the local shopping centre. You can cover a lot of distance on one of these expeditions and never even notice the effort. Whether you are shopping, working or visiting friends, make it a habit to take the stairs. You can build your aerobic ability while you develop the strength in your legs and tone your tummy. Around the house, pick up your pace while doing chores so you can burn some excess calories and finish your tasks sooner—leaving more time for fun.

Your Fitness Strengths and Weaknesses

Your astro-symbol, the Archer, represents your desire and ability to hit your marks in life, so once you put your mind to something, there's nothing stopping you! Regardless of how big or small your fitness goals are, you have what it takes to make it happen and you know how to have fun while doing it! I should caution that Sagittarians can be prone to inflammation and injuries, especially around the ankles, knees and shoulders. To sidestep these potential problems, avoid high-impact aerobics and other activities that can over-stress these joints.

Fitness Tips

Fill your calendar with activities you love to do and don't sit around the house when you're bored. Boredom is a high calorie emotion for a Sagittarian and it can lead to binge eating—simply because you don't have anything more appealing to do. An Archer's appetite can be as insatiable as your curiosity, so avoid situations where you will be surrounded by food and opt for circumstances where you can feed your inquiring mind instead.

How to Reward Yourself

With the planet Jupiter ruling your sign, you thrive on fast action and fast rewards! Even instant gratification sometimes takes too long as far as you're concerned. You set your aims high, so make sure you break down your goals into small steps. Assign rewards for each step and then chart your progress and celebrate your fitness accomplishments with well-deserved rewards.

Capricorn

Bend and stretch, touch your toes and reach for the shelves while you're shopping, putting away the groceries, or checking out the new releases at the video store. As a Capricorn, you hold most of your stress and tension in your back and shoulders so gentle stretching will reduce your aches and pains and make you more flexible. Consciously increase your bending and stretching while making beds, tending to the garden or mowing the lawn. Stop, take a deep breath, and gently bend down towards your toes a few times throughout the day. Wherever possible, walk instead of driving and make a special effort to enjoy the fresh air and scenery at a leisurely pace, rather than rushing.

Your Fitness Strengths and Weaknesses

Like the hardy Goat that is your astro-symbol, yours is one of the physically stronger signs. You also have staying power and determination so you can reach all of your fitness goals if you are persistent. Take good care of your knees and avoid potential joint problems with low impact exercises such as swimming, walking and cycling. Steer away from high heels! These fashion favourites can throw your delicate back out badly.

Fitness Tips

Avoid overdoing it with heavy lifting or pushing yourself too hard. Just because you can do something, doesn't mean you should! Combine sport with socialising by joining a recreational sports team or athletic club. Team sports are really good for you because they help you to create a routine. Arrange outings with friends and family in parks or recreational settings, rather than meeting for lunch, dinner or parties that involve rich, fattening foods.

How to Reward Yourself

As a Capricorn, you're notorious for accomplishing one goal and moving right on to the next without rewarding yourself. Assign rewards to your specific goals, and make sure your goals are set in small increments so you can reap a self-promised reward every week or so. One of the best gifts you can give yourself is 'personal time' to unwind, pamper yourself, read something fun (self-improvement articles don't count!), take a nap, or just stare out of the window and enjoy a great daydream.

Aquarius

Surprises and unexpected events are par for the course for an Aquarian, so tap into your creativity for a wide variety of ways to mix fun fitness with whatever else is happening in your life. Since you are naturally innovative, be on the lookout for new ways to accomplish old tasks by tossing some fun into everyday hum-drum chores. Play 'beat the clock' by cleaning the house in hyperspeed and get a great aerobic work-out at the same time. Stretch your leg and back muscles by bending over at the waist to pick up items from the floor or low shelves and keep it up until you can easily touch your toes without bending your knees. March your garbage bags to the curb for pick-up and use some elbow grease to scrub away the bath tub ring.

Your Fitness Strengths and Weaknesses

Your sign is blessed with strength and vitality and with a moderate amount of exercise, sunshine and fresh air, you can take on any challenge. Get into the habit of stretching your calf muscles and propping your feet up when you're resting because Aquarians sometimes have problems with their shins and ankles and can be susceptible to varicose veins. Avoid sitting in one position for long periods, particularly with one leg crossed over the other. It is important for you to use caution when you're exercising or playing sports because you can be accident-prone when your mind wanders or drifts into a daydream.

Fitness Tips

Sleepless nights, allergy attacks or stomach disorders are sometimes signs that you have excess tension that needs to be released, or you're overdoing it with too much physical exertion. Your system responds to all forms of fitness and the key for you is to gradually increase your heart rate to improve your circulation. When you have a bit of free time, get some extra exercise by dancing, sightseeing or photographing interesting or beautiful aspects of your neighbourhood or surrounding areas. When it's time to rest, lie in the sun, breathe deeply, and practise yoga or meditation. This will support all your efforts in reaching a higher level of fitness.

How to Reward Yourself

Going new places, trying out the latest trends and shopping for unique novelties in bohemian-style shops all make an Aquarian's heart beat a little faster. Reward yourself with tickets to alternative music concerts, hit the hottest dance clubs, and see the controversial art exhibits and films that might be shocking for others, but are perfect for your uncommon tastes. Another great reward for a Water-bearer is a day of total leisure, where you have no goals whatsoever and drift wherever the energy of the day takes you.

Pisces

The routine and discipline often demanded to maintain ongoing optimum physical fitness for the active nature and easily distracted personality of Pisces do not really go together. Pisces love to think more about exercise than actually doing it. Extremes often apply to this sign and you will find some Pisceans who are fitness fanatics and always in the pool or at the gym, and others who are totally disinterested in any form of exercise. Some Pisceans go through extreme cycles of both trends, devotedly exercising for months and then completely stopping.

Usually the dreamy influence of the planet Neptune can make it difficult for Pisceans to get motivated where fitness is concerned. That is why it is more important for you, than for most signs, to really have fun with fitness and to gradually make it a part of the everyday. And you do not have to join the gym to do this. Start slowly by parking your car at the furthest end of the car park at work, at appointments, at meetings or at shopping centres, and get off the bus a few blocks before your destination. Join an athletic club and meet your clients and friends on the golf course, at the pool, or on the running track, instead of at a nearby restaurant. When you're at home, keep yourself moving by setting a deadline for getting the housework done and put some muscle into scouring the pots and pans, shaking out the sheets and towels, and removing spots from rugs and furniture.

Your Fitness Strengths and Weaknesses

The old Zen saying, 'If the shoe fits, the foot is forgotten', was written with Pisces in mind. A Piscean woman can have the most beautiful feet, with dainty polished toenails at the end of perfectly shaped toes, however, these ultra-feminine foundations are quite sensitive and can be prone to aches, bunions and corns. It is of paramount importance to wear the right kind of shoes that treat your feet kindly. In addition, wherever possible, wear low rather than high heels. Whether at home, work or out socialising, go for a style of shoe that feels comfortable. The wrong shoe will make you miserable and could even lead to chronic foot or back problems over the long term. Look for opportunities to go barefoot and make it a habit to slip out of your shoes and into cosy slippers or therapeutic sandals when you are at home.

Fitness Tips

Your ruling planet, Neptune, is the ancient god of the sea, so you're naturally drawn to water. Outdoor activities such as swimming, surfing and water-skiing are fun ways for you to bump up your fitness level without much effort. You'll feel more alert and have extra energy for a walk or a swim after work if you cash in your afternoon coffee break for a cup of stimulating herbal tea, such as peppermint, ginseng or ginger.

How to Reward Yourself

Book yourself in for a pedicure or a foot massage (also known as reflexology). Aromatherapy is also very relaxing and healing for you. A gentle or deep massage not only soothes the body, but also the mind and soul. As a reward, at least once a week, play soft music, fill your bathroom with scented candles, pour oil into the bath and enjoy a private moment of solitude. When you reach a major goal, treat yourself to a full day or weekend package at a health spa.

Appendix
More Psychic Tests and Exercises

Now that you can recognise which psychic senses you may fall under, the following section provides some questionnaires and exercises to help you discover the depth of your psychic abilities—the actual strength of your powers. This is another good way to discover whether you are tapping into the psychic flow or not.

Discovering How Psychic You Are

Utilising the YES or NO question and answer method, answer the following questionnaire to determine whether you are using any psychic powers in your life. The more 'Yes' answers you have, the more powerful are your psychic powers.

1. Have you ever made a wish and then seen it occur almost before your eyes, as if by magic?
2. Have you ever thought of someone, only to hear the phone ring and when you answered it the person you had been thinking of was on the other end of the line?
3. Have you called someone, only to find out that they were picking up the phone at that instant to call you?

4. Have you been humming or whistling a tune and then turned on your radio only to hear it playing at exactly the same tune?

5. How many times have you asked yourself a most unusual question like, 'I wonder how many miles away the Moon is?' only to turn on the television or radio and hear the response 'The Moon is...miles away from Earth'? Or have you picked up a magazine or book and it has the information you wanted right before your eyes?

6. Have you thought about someone you haven't seen about for many years, and then suddenly bump into them on the street, or has another person told you news about this individual straight after you 'thought' about them?

7. Have you ever been in someone's company and both said exactly the same thing at the very same time in an 'out of the blue' fashion that caught you both by surprise?

8. Have you visited a close friend or family member only to find that when you arrived at their house they had purchased something exactly the same as you had recently?

9. Have you accidentally encountered someone from your past only to discover that amazing coincidences in dates, places or people ran through both of your lives (i.e. you both had a child born on the same day which you had given the same name, or got married to your partners on the same day, etc?).

10. Have some of the most profound events in your life, such as the way you met your partner, been so fateful that they appear to be designed by destiny?

11. Have you had a strong instinct about something which you ignored, only to find out later that your instinct was right and you made a mistake not to heed it?

12. Have you lost something only to find it again a long time later under the most bizarre conditions?
13. Have you ever awoken in the morning with a 'sense' that something wonderful (or something ominous) was going to occur during that day...and it did?
14. Have you ever had a sense that danger was around you when doing something (for example, like driving a car), so you took precautionary measures (i.e., slowed down or changed course) and you saved yourself from grief?
15. Have you ever gone to bed at night worried about a problem and woken the next morning knowing that something was going to happen to resolve the problem, and that something had occurred?

The Willpower Magic Energy Ritual

The Willpower Magic Energy Ritual is an energy exercise I perform every day for myself. It is like spending time doing a meditation or some self-hypnosis, and I truly believe that it has worked miracles in my life. It is very simple to do and requires just a few minutes of your time. It is also lots of fun! It develops disciplines (if you do it regularly) that can help you remember to watch out for the enemies that encourage you to put on weight, or slip from your healthy lifestyle. I use this willpower magic energy ritual to keep me focused on upgrading my life on all levels (not just for staying thin).

To perform the Willpower Magic Energy Ritual, stand in front of a full-length mirror, in a position where you can see your entire body—from the top of your head to the tips of your toes, either fully clothed or naked. I personally do it straight after I have a shower in the morning, because I think it is wise to start the day with fresh energy and the willpower magic energy gets my day off to a great start. I also perform this exercise whenever it is possible throughout the day, and at night before I retire. However, just once a day is enough if that's all the time you have, but if you do find your willpower is slipping—the more you can do this exercise, the less likely you will fall into temptation.

To do this exercise you will need:

• a single white candle in a candle stand
• a match or lighter to light the candle
• a candle snuffer.

Once you have positioned yourself in front of the mirror, light the candle, which will commence the magic energy, and look at yourself in the mirror, seeing yourself as beautiful in your mind's eye. Then recite the following magic energy incantation three times:

Mirror, mirror on the wall,
My willpower is growing and encompassing all,
My powerful magic will see me succeed and shine,
My willpower is empowered and my life now divine.
So be it!

Say this incantation aloud, and when you say the words, express yourself confidently and put true intent and meaning behind the words. That is, when you say the magic energy incantation, say it as if you really mean what you are saying.

Don't be half-hearted. Speak from the heart and with power behind your words. When you complete the magic energy, snuff out the candle with a candle snuffer or with dampened fingers (do not blow out the candle with your breath, as that destroys the power of the magic energy). The snuffing out of the candle's flame completes the process.

The Magic Wheel of Willpower (the quick-fix to recharging your willpower)

When you are on the run and caught up in a busy day, you will discover that there is insufficient time to do the Willpower Magic Energy Ritual set out previously. So here's a quick-fix energiser for your willpower—The Magic Wheel of Willpower—which provides you with something that you can carry with you wherever you go. You will find a diagram of The Magic Wheel of Willpower on the next page. Once you get into the habit of using it, you will discover that when you boost your willpower, you immediately gain more control over what you eat—and therefore have the inner power to lose weight or give up bad habits.

Here is all you need to do. Just put your right palm on the Magic Wheel of Willpower (or your left palm if you are left-handed) and relax. Let your mind tap into the willpower of higher power that surrounds this Wheel of Willpower. You don't have to do or think anything—just use the wheel as a mental willpower energy charger (like plugging into a willpower battery). You may feel a tingle or other sensation in your palm

The Magic Wheel of Willpower

but the main thing is to feel strengthened and empowered. Leave your palm on the wheel of willpower for a moment, or several minutes. Let the force flow through you. Use it as often as you feel drawn to using it—it will help you strengthen your resolve and put you back on the right track of life again (particularly when you feel you might be straying or have lost your way). This wheel is different from the Lucky Magic Star at the beginning of this book, because the star is something that you make wishes upon, whereas this wheel of willpower is something you extract uplifting energy from. The star is something you put energy into (you put your wish energy into it to make your wishes come true). The Wheel of Willpower is a tool for boosting your willpower energies so you are no longer affected by outside temptations. You become the controller of your own destiny and that is something to celebrate!

In the previous pages, I have shared with you many powerful mental exercises and practical insights. I know these methods work because I have tried and tested them myself and have reaped their benefits. If you have read this far, you should now have sufficient knowledge to move into the future with a new vision of yourself and what you can accomplish. And, if some things do not happen overnight for you, do not falter. Some results take longer than others to attain—but when you persist and put your mind to work (instead of allowing your random thinking processes to run you in confused circles), you'll be amazed at the magnificent world you suddenly discover exists within and around you.

So, it is time now to go out and live your highest dreams in your own inimitable style. Enjoy the wonderful journey awaiting you and let your mind become your magic carpet that transports you to wherever you want to be or whatever you want to do.

Big hug,
Athena

About Athena Starwoman

Born from a long line of mystics and astrologers, Athena is well-known internationally as one of the world's leading astrologers. Athena's regular zodiac columns appear in *Vogue* (USA), *The Australian Women's Weekly* (Australia), *Star Magazine* (USA), and *Elegance* (Holland). She has also written the astrology books *Zodiac*, *Zodiac Lovers* and *Soulmates and the Zodiac,* and in conjunction with her friend Deborah Gray, a magical spell book entitled *How to Turn Your Ex-boyfriend into a Toad* and a guide to glamour called *Glamazon: How to be fabulous, famous and flawless*.

Married to American inspirational speaker, Dr John F Demartini, both Athena and John lead a jet set gypsy existence commuting from John's head office in Houston, Texas to their 'temple-like' penthouse on the Gold Coast of Australia. Always on the go, the two are either exploring or returning to somewhere special around the globe. Since it's launch in Oslo in March 2002, Athena now calls the luxury residential ship *The World* her home. Residing in an apartment on board, she sails into New York, Monte Carlo or the wonderlands of Iceland, St Petersburg or Alaska, writing her columns and books on the seven oceans of the world.

Through her astrological, psychic and mystical columns and features, Athena has already helped many to rediscover their own power, through mastering the ancient mental sacred sciences.

You can find out more about Athena on her website at www.athenastarwoman.com.